Pupil's Book 4

Barry and Anita Scholes

CollinsEducational
An Imprint of HarperCollins*Publishers*

Notes for the teacher

Collins Primary English Pupil's Book 4 consists of 17 four-page units, and 1 six-page unit covering reading, writing and language study. The units also offer frequent opportunities for the development of talking, speaking and listening skills. Unit 18 gives an opportunity for the assessment of the children's progress. There is a three-page reference section at the back of the book with a glossary of language terms and guidance on the writing process, how to find and use information and how to use the Look, Cover, Remember, Write, Check method for spellings. Please encourage the children to use these pages whenever such help is needed.

Skills Workbooks 4A and 4B link closely with the pupil's book to help develop the children's understanding of spelling, punctuation and the structure, vocabulary and grammar of Standard English. It is not intended that the workbooks should be worked through independently of the pupil's book. The two workbooks have been designed to complement the pupil's book, and pupils should work only the pages linked to the current pupil's book unit. The teacher's notes have advice on how to use the notebooks in this way.

Please note that the workbook material for Unit 10 is split between Workbook 4A (page 24) and Workbook 4B (pages 2-4). Teacher's Resource Book 4 explains how to integrate the different components of Collins Primary English. It offers advice on how the pupil's book may be used, and gives ideas for consolidation and extension activities.

Copymasters in the Teacher's Resource Book 4 consolidate and extend the work in the pupil's book. In several cases they have been designed specifically to help structure response to the pupil's book activities, thus giving the teacher the flexibility to differentiate work by offering more or less help to individuals. Occasionally an activity sheet may be necessary for all pupils. Other copymasters cover listening skills, record keeping, presentation and self assessment.

Cassette 4 features a range of activities to help develop listening skills. The tracks are linked to copymasters which cover a variety of responses. The tape may be listened to by a group or individually, at the teacher's discretion.

A note on differentiation

The pupil's books and the cassette are suitable for a wide ability range, with greater or lesser help required from the teacher according to the needs of the children. Differentiation here will depend mainly on outcome and the amount of help given.

The copymasters feature a range of follow-up activities for consolidation and extension, offering opportunities for differentiation by task. It should be noted, however, that for some children many of these activities in Collins Primary English will not depend on a written outcome and much of the learning can come from discussion and interaction with the teacher.

Contents

About Me

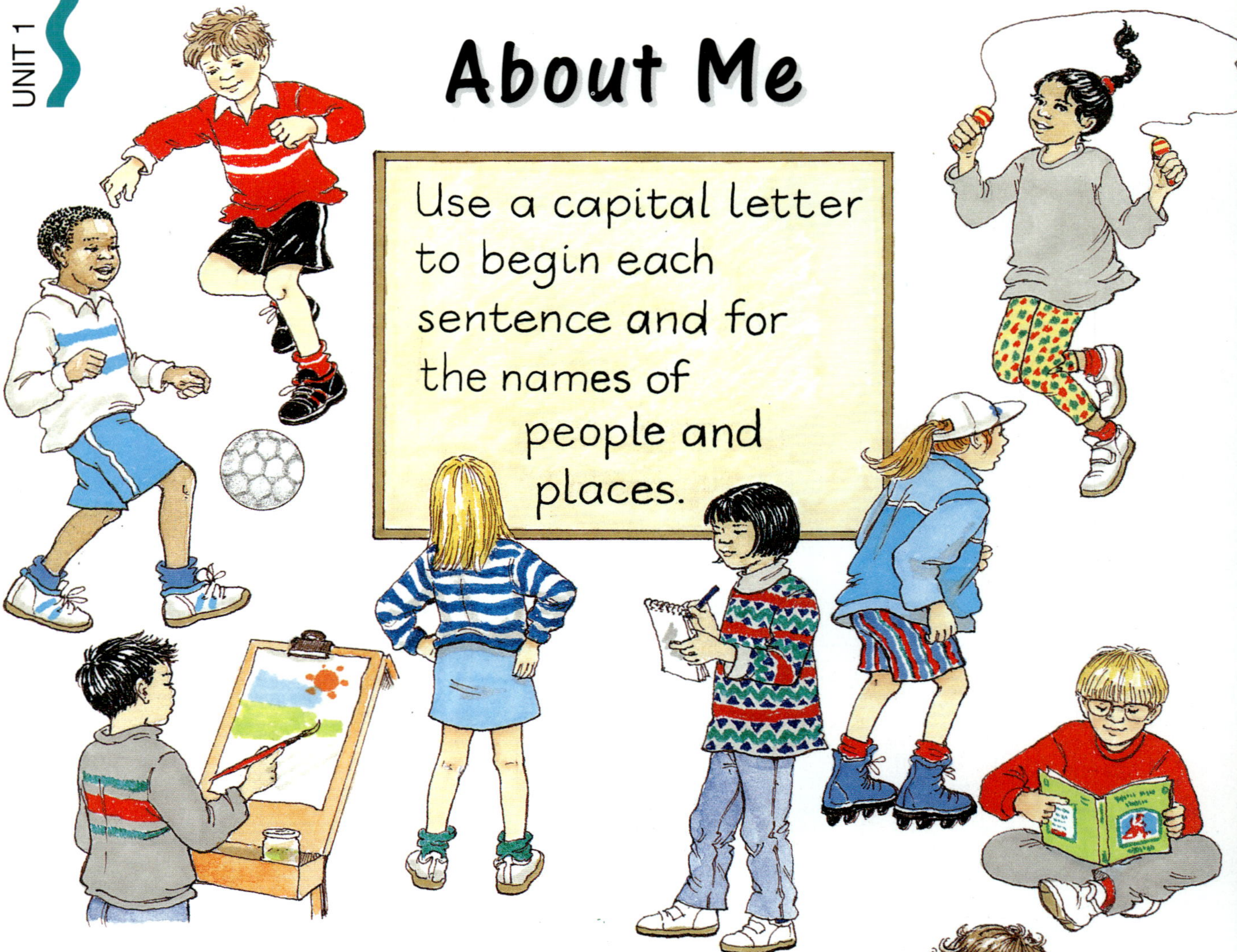

A Myself

My name is Daniel Andrews. I am nine years old. I have brown eyes and dark brown curly hair. I live with my mother and my younger sister Lindsey. My favourite clothes are jeans and a T shirt. My favourite food is hamburger and chips. My favourite book is *Harry's Mad* by Dick King-Smith. The TV programme I like best is Cartoon Time. I go to Westhill School. I am best at English and Science, but I would like to be better at Maths. On Saturdays I usually play football with my friends. On Sundays I visit grandma and grandad.

Write a description of yourself like the one Daniel wrote. Add anything else you think is interesting about yourself. Then draw a picture of yourself and your family.

Writing a diary

This is Amanda's diary. In it she wrote down what she did and how she felt.

Monday	We won at rounders today. I felt happy.
Tuesday	I went to the dentist for a check up. I was worried, but when he told me my teeth were fine I felt great!
Wednesday	We had a maths test today. I didn't do very well. I'm not pleased with myself.
Thursday	Today I swam for the first time. It was just a few strokes, but my teacher says I am now a swimmer. I can't wait for next week!
Friday	It was hot and sunny all day today. I hope it stays the same for the weekend.
Saturday	We went to the seaside with Auntie Aisha, Uncle James and Jenny. We had a wonderful time. Jenny and I collected some beautiful sea shells.
Sunday	I helped Mum and Dad with the cooking. I made a cake which we ate for tea. It was delicious.

B About Amanda's diary

1. On which day did Amanda have a maths test?
   Begin: Amanda had a maths test on...
2. Where did she go on Saturday?
3. How did she feel before she went to the dentist?
4. How did she feel afterwards? Why do you think so?
5. What did she do at the seaside?
6. Which do you think was her most special day? Why do you think so?

C Your special day

Write about a special day you can remember.
Ask yourself: What happened? How did I feel? How did the day end?

D Your own diary

Write your own diary for a week.
Ask yourself: What did I do? Who with? How did I feel?

About Me
Friends

Friends

I'll read with you, and play with you,
I'll sit in school all day with you,
I'll give you my best Lego set,
I'll do your writing, so you'll get
A gold star, and my car I'll lend
To you 'cause you're my best, best friend.

Theresa Heine

Think about your best friend. Ask yourself these questions.

- What does my friend look like?
- What does my friend do?
- What sort of things do we do together?
- What does my friend like or dislike?
- How do I feel about my friend?
- What special things would I do for my friend?

Hannah thought about her best friend.
These are some of the notes she made.

What does she look like? Tall, blue eyes, short fair hair, always smiling. What does she do? Giggles a lot, hardly ever stops talking.

This is how she used her notes to begin a description of her friend.

My friend Stacey is tall. She has blue eyes and short fair hair. There is always a smile on her face and she often breaks into a fit of giggles. She hardly ever seems to stop talking.

Make similar notes about your best friend.
Then use your notes to write a full description.

Names

A Alphabetical order

These are the names of all Hannah's friends. Write them in alphabetical order.

Stacey	Amy	Lauren
Sita	Lee	Vicky
Mark	Ryan	Rachel

B Telephone directory

In a telephone directory names are listed in alphabetical order of a person's surname. This is part of a telephone directory Hannah made of her friends and relatives.

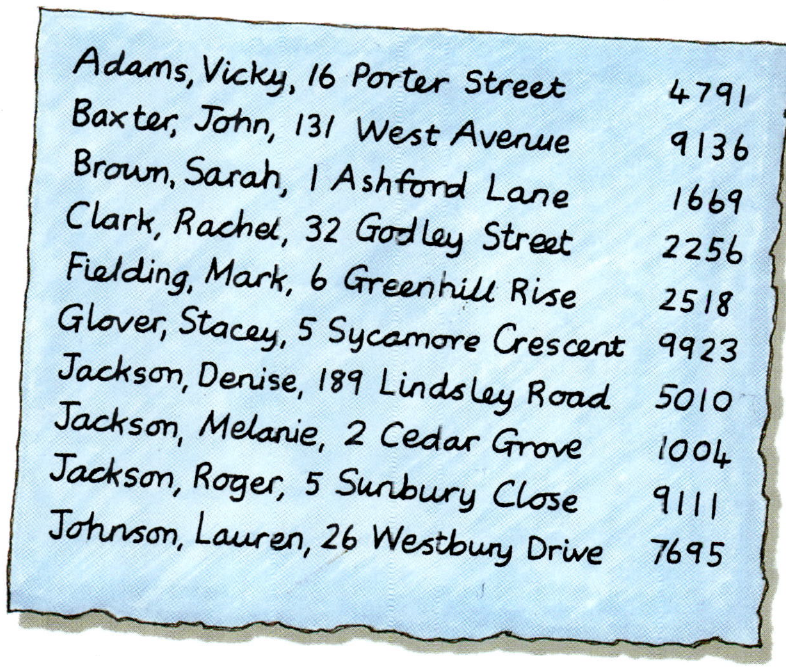

Adams, Vicky, 16 Porter Street	4791
Baxter, John, 131 West Avenue	9136
Brown, Sarah, 1 Ashford Lane	1669
Clark, Rachel, 32 Godley Street	2256
Fielding, Mark, 6 Greenhill Rise	2518
Glover, Stacey, 5 Sycamore Crescent	9923
Jackson, Denise, 189 Lindsley Road	5010
Jackson, Melanie, 2 Cedar Grove	1004
Jackson, Roger, 5 Sunbury Close	9111
Johnson, Lauren, 26 Westbury Drive	7695

Use Hannah's telephone directory to answer these questions.

1. Write down the telephone numbers of these people.
   a) Rachel Clark
   b) Stacey Glover
   c) Sarah Brown
   d) Roger Jackson
2. Write down the addresses of these people.
   a) Lauren Johnson
   b) John Baxter
   c) Melanie Jackson
   d) Vicky Adams
3. Whose telephone numbers are these?
   a) 1669
   b) 5010
   c) 9923
   d) 9111
   e) 2518

C Your own telephone directory

Make a telephone directory of your friends and relatives.

D The name game

Play with your name like this. Each line of your poem should say something about the person.

Stacey Glover
Smiles Giggles
Skipping Game
Sweet Grapes
Super Girl

Now do the same with your best friend's name.

Feelings

To Beat a Bad Temper

An angry tiger in a cage
Will roar and roar and roar with rage,
And gnash his teeth and lash his tail.
For that's how tigers rant and rail.
I keep my temper in a cage,
I hate it when it roars with rage,
I hate its teeth, I hate its tail,
So when it starts to rant and rail,
I tell my mum, I tell my dad,
I tell them why it's feeling bad,
And then I skip and skip and skip,
And lash my rope just like a whip,
And when I skip because I'm cross,
My temper-tiger knows who's boss,
And when I've skipped and whipped
  like mad,
My temper-tiger's not so bad.
I have to keep it tame this way,
Or it will eat me up one day.

Cynthia Mitchell

A

1. What animal does the poet say her temper is like?
   Begin: The poet says her temper is like a...
2. What do you think 'rant and rail' means?
3. What does she do when she gets in a temper?
4. What might happen if she did not control her temper?
5. What do you do when you have a bad temper?
6. What animal is your temper like?

B

Write about a time when you had a bad temper.
What made you angry?
What did you do?
What did other people do?
How did you eventually beat your temper?
How did you feel afterwards?

C Feelings as colours

When we are sad we sometimes say we feel blue. What colour might you feel if you were:

a) angry?
b) happy?
c) bored?
d) afraid?
e) sleepy?
f) excited?
g) calm?

D Writing a poem

Happiness

Happiness is as yellow as the summer sun,
It tastes of lemonade, sweet and tingly.
It smells of cake cooking in the oven,
And sounds like laughter at a birthday party.
It feels warm and soft and cuddly.

Make a list of all the different feelings you can think of. Choose one of these for a poem of your own.
Make notes about it using this formula.

- What colour is this feeling?
- What does it taste like?
- What does it smell like?
- What does it sound like?
- What does it feel like?

Use your notes and the formula to write your poem.

Feelings

Never Kiss Frogs!

Gail had a funny habit. She tried to kiss frogs. She would get down on her hands and knees and put her face up close, but at that point they always jumped away. Until…

One day, Gail had a row with her mother. She went out into the garden for a sulk. There'd been a shower and the sun had just come out again. Everything was damp and steamy. As Gail got to the bottom of the garden and looked round for something to kick, she suddenly had the feeling that someone was was watching her. She looked around – there was no one there. But Gail knew she was being watched.

Then she saw it. Sitting under a dock leaf, big beady eyes staring, breathing in and out, was the biggest, fattest, grottiest frog. For a moment or two they looked at each other, then the frog spoke.

'Sweet lady. Please have pity on me.'

'You what?' said Gail. She didn't mean to be rude. Her mother was always trying to get her to say 'Beg pardon'. But it just came out.

'Have pity on a poor creature in distress,' said the frog.

Gail crouched down and put her face a few inches from the frog's. But it didn't move. Instead it spoke again.

'My story,' said the frog, 'is a long and sad one…'

But Gail couldn't wait. She knew what she had to do. She squeezed up her mouth and gave the frog a great big kiss right in the middle of his sentence.

From *Never Kiss Frogs!* by Robert Leeson

A

1. How do you know Gail was in a bad mood that day?
   Begin: I know Gail was in a bad mood that day because…
2. Why did she look around?
3. Where was the frog?
4. Why do you think Gail was rude to him?
5. Why didn't she wait for the frog to finish his story?

B

1. Why do you think Gail wanted to kiss frogs?
2. What sad story might the frog have told if Gail had given him the chance?
3. Why do you think the author says she kissed him 'right in the middle of his sentence'?
4. What do you think will happen next?

C

Read these two sentences. The words in bold type in the second sentence are adjectives.

The adjectives help us to imagine the frog much more clearly.

Rewrite the passage below. Think of at least one interesting adjective for each of the underlined nouns. Help your reader to see a clear picture in his imagination.

At the top of the street was a house with a garden. Under a tree in the garden was a pool where a frog lived under a stone.

Planning

The best stories always have a problem for the main character to overcome. What problem might result when Gail kisses the frog?

- How might the frog change?
- How might Gail change?
- How will she feel about what happens?
- How will the story turn out in the end?

D

Continue the story of Gail and the frog. Choose interesting adjectives.

Talking

A cartoon strip is one way of showing people talking.

Another way is to write it as a play.

Boy	Knock, knock!
Girl	Who's there?
Boy	Ken.
Girl	Ken who?
Boy	Ken I come in?

Read this cartoon strip.

A

Write the words of this cartoon as a play.

B

Write a **Knock, knock!** joke of your own, first as a cartoon strip, and then as a play.

The Gold Jug

Read both versions of this story.

The Gold Jug

Characters:
Martin, a schoolboy
Rachel, Martin's sister

Scene:
Beside a canal

Martin What's that?
Rachel Where?
Martin There. It looks like a gold jug!
Rachel You're right.
Martin I think I can reach it.
Rachel Do be careful!
Martin Oh!
(He falls in the water.)

Look at how the play is set out. It has a **title**, a **list of characters**, and describes the **scene**, or setting, where the story takes place. **Actions** are shown in brackets on a separate line.

C

1. Copy the play in your best handwriting.
2. Think what might happen next. How will Martin get out of the water? Will he need to be rescued? Does he get the jug? Is the jug what it appears to be? Write your own ending to the play.

Talking

What People Really Say

People do not really talk like that, do they? This is what they would really say:

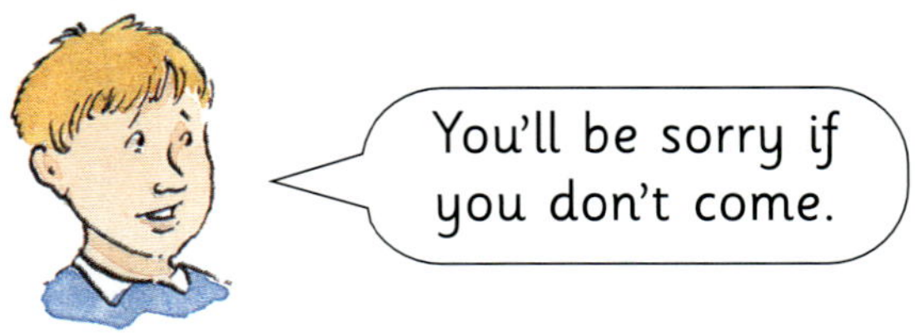

When people speak they use short forms of some words.

you will = you'll   I am = I'm   cannot = can't   he would = he'd

The apostrophe, or raised comma, shows us where one or more letters have been missed out.

you'will   she'is   they'are

Important!
In writing we use short forms only for words that are spoken, or when writing a letter to a friend.

A

Write the full form of these.

1. don't
2. he's
3. you're
4. I'll
5. who's
6. wouldn't
7. isn't
8. I've
9. we've
10. it'll

B

Write the short form of these.

1. she is
2. they are
3. he will
4. cannot
5. we will
6. they will
7. you will
8. I shall
9. do not
10. it is

C

Write these sentences giving the short forms in full.

1. We're going to town, but we can't stay long.
2. He'll be pleased we've bought him a present.
3. I'm sure they'll be here soon.
4. I've no idea why she didn't do it. Perhaps she couldn't.

D

Imagine you are Martin or Rachel in the story on page 13. Write a letter to a friend saying what happened. Use the short forms you would use in speech.

Exclamations

Look at the exclamation mark at the end of Martin's sentence. An exclamation mark is a kind of exciting full stop. We use it to show surprise, or for commands and warnings:

Rewrite the sentences which need an exclamation mark.

Come back	Where are you going	Look out	I like adventure stories
Oh no, I've broken my pencil	It's a goal	It's two o'clock	Help

Conversations

What do you think these people will say next?
Choose one of the situations.
Work with a friend and make notes of your ideas.
Then talk to each other as if you are the characters. Write your conversation as a play.

Food

'Arthur,' said Mrs. Crocodile to her son one evening at dinner, 'you are eating like a regular little beast.'

'He won't close his mouth when he chews,' said Arthur's sister, Emma, 'and I have to sit opposite him, so I have a good view of everything.'

'Whuzzhuh maher?' said Arthur.

'Don't talk when your mouth is full,' said Father. 'Little bits of ravioli are landing on your sister and no one can understand what you are saying.'

'It's awful,' said Emma.

'It certainly is,' said Mother.

'Everybody always picks on me,' said Arthur when his mouth was empty.

From *Dinner at Alberta's* by Russell Hoban and James Marshall

A About the story

1. What was Arthur eating?
2. Why did Emma object to the way Arthur was eating?
3. What were Father's two objections?
4. Why is it amusing that Mrs. Crocodile should say he was eating 'like a regular little beast'?
5. How did Arthur feel about these remarks?
6. When Arthur said 'Whuzzhuh maher?', what was he trying to say?

B Reading for clues

Think for yourself what the missing words are. The clues are in the meaning of the passage, so read each sentence carefully. Copy the passage, putting one word for each space.

Arthur had very ____①___ table manners. He talked with his ____②___ full. This annoyed his ____③___, Emma. It annoyed his mother and ____④___ too. Arthur was tired of being told ____⑤___. He said that everybody was ____⑥___ on him.

Words of similar meaning

devour

nibble

slurp

gulp

Look at these words for different ways of eating and drinking.

eat

taste	gobble	dine
devour	chew	graze
nibble	munch	feed

drink

sip	gulp
guzzle	slurp
lap	suck

C Copy and complete

Choose a suitable word to complete these sentences.

1. Don't ________ your soup so noisily!
2. _______ the stew to see if it needs more salt.
3. They watch the cows _______ on the sweet grass.
4. The cats _______ the milk from the saucer.
5. He had to _______ the tough meat for a long time.
6. I'm so hungry I could _______ up all of the cakes.

D Giant Greedy Guts

Choose suitable words for how Giant Greedy Guts would eat and drink.

E Writing sentences

Use each of these words in a sentence of your own to show its meaning.

1. bite	2. crunchy	3. barbecue	4. swallow
5. sour	6. vinegar	7. nasty	8. lick

F Using a thesaurus

Use a thesaurus to find as many words as you can which are similar in meaning to the word **cook**. Use each word in a sentence of your own.

Food
Delicious

Why do you think the second stall is selling more apples?

A Adjectives add flavour

Add adjectives of your own to make these foods sound delicious. Here are some to start you off.

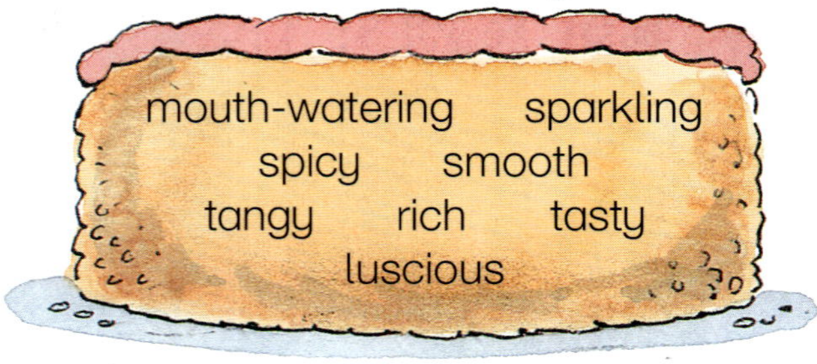

1. oranges
2. ice cream
3. breakfast cereal
4. cake
5. soup
6. fruit juice
7. chocolate
8. potato crisps

B Giving instructions

1. These instructions for making a sandwich are mixed up. Write them in the correct order.

   How to make a peanut butter sandwich
   - Spread butter on each slice.
   - Cut the sandwich in two. Enjoy.
   - Spread the peanut butter on one slice.
   - Take two slices of bread.
   - Put the two slices together.

2. Write instructions for making any two of these.
   a) your favourite sandwich
   b) an ice lolly
   c) a cup of tea or coffee
   d) a milk shake

Sweet Song

This is the sweet song,
Song of all the sweets,
Caramel and butterscotch
Bullseyes, raspberry treats;

Treacle toffee, acid drops,
Pastilles, crystal fruits,
Bubble-gum and liquorice sticks
As black as new gum-boots;

Peppermint creams and aniseed balls,
Tiny sweets and whoppers,
Dolly-mixtures, chocolate drops,
Gigantic gob-stoppers;

Lemon sherbets, jelly babies,
Chocolate cream and flake,
Nougat, fudge and such as give
You tooth and belly-ache.

Vernon Scannell

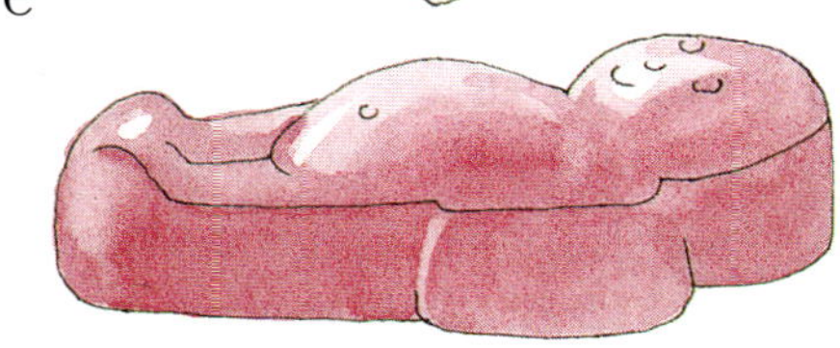

C About the poem

1. Which is your favourite sweet? Say why.
2. Are there any you don't like? Say why.
3. In what way are liquorice sticks like new gum-boots?
4. What are the dangers of eating too many of these sweets?

D Writing a poem

Write your own poem about food using this one as a model.
Begin like this:

> This is the food song,
> Song of all the treats,
> Breakfast, tea and dinner time,
> Main course, lovely sweets.

Planning

First make a list of foods. Your poem does not have to rhyme, but if you want rhymes then match up rhyming pairs first. Your rhyming words should go at the end of lines 2 and 4 in each verse.
Here are some rhymes to start you off:

jam – lamb
fish – dish
crunchy – munchy
cakes – corn flakes
meat – shredded wheat

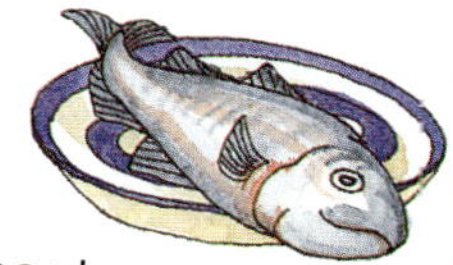

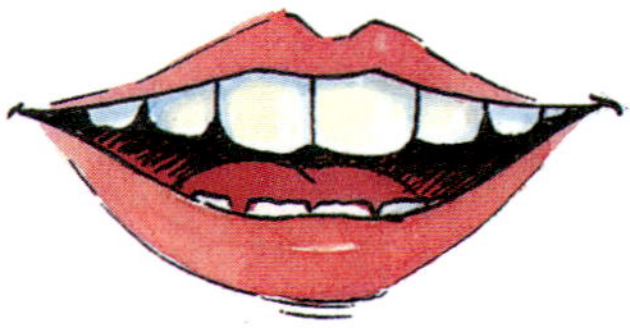

Teeth

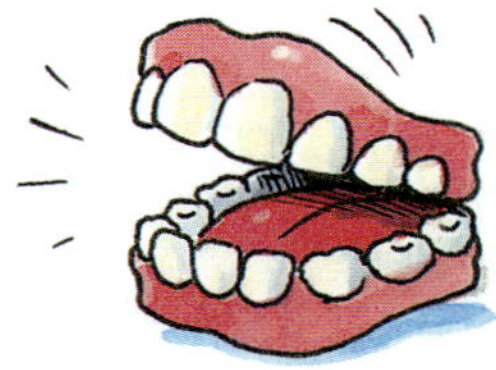

Elizabeth had never been to the dentist before. She was not sure what one was supposed to go to the dentist for. She was a little frightened and yet still excited at the thought of the visit.

'Will the dentist make my mouth stop hurting?' she asked her mother who was busy clearing away the breakfast things.

'Hope so,' Elizabeth's mother said, taking away Elizabeth's boiled egg before she had even cracked it. 'He may take out de toof dat hurting.'

'I don't want him to take out the tooth. I want it to fall out by itself so that I can put it under my pillow then the tooth fairy can take it away and leave a silver coin... like Alicia's fairy at school,' she sulked.

'Alicia's fairy? her mother asked.

'Yes,' Elizabeth said, remembering what her friend Alicia had told her when her tooth had fallen out.

'The tooth fairy comes in the middle of the night and takes the tooth to the pearl palace where all the teeth that have fallen out are polished up and made magic.'

'I see,' said Elizabeth's mother. 'Perhaps if you ax him nicely de dentis' will give you back de toof to take home wid you.'

'I'll ax him nicely,' Elizabeth said, feeling better already.

From *Mammy, Sugar Falling Down* by Trish Cooke

A About the story

1. What time of day was it? How do you know?
2. Why did Elizabeth want her tooth to fall out by itself?
3. What had Alicia told her about the tooth fairy?
4. What did Elizabeth's mother say to make her feel better?

B To write about

Write about your first visit to the dentist.
Why did you go?
How did you feel before you went?
What happened there?
How did you feel afterwards?

C Reading for clues

The story of Elizabeth's tooth is continued here. Think for yourself what the missing words are. The clues are in the meaning of the passage, so read each sentence carefully. Copy the passage, putting one word for each space.

When Elizabeth and her mother were ____①___ at the bus stop, Elizabeth saw the O'Brian twins. The O'Brian ____②___ sat at the back of her classroom. Elizabeth tied her scarf tighter around her ____③___ for greater effect.

'Hello Kerrie, ___④___ Robert,' she said loudly, so they would not miss her under the red ___⑤___.

'I'm going to the ____⑥___,' she yelled, and then she covered her face quickly because cold air had got into her ___⑦___ bringing with it a sharp pain that tingled at her gums.

The parts of a tooth

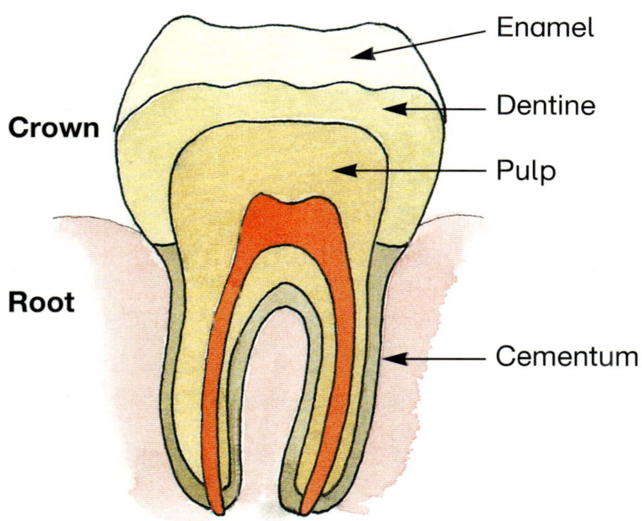

The **crown** is the part of the tooth we can see. The **root** is the part under the gum. **Enamel** is the hard, shiny covering for the crown. Most of the inside of the tooth consists of **dentine**. It is not as hard as enamel. The **pulp** is soft. It is the living part of the tooth. **Cementum** is hard and holds the tooth in place.

D

1. What do we call the **part of the tooth** we can see?
2. What is the part **under the gum**?
3. What is **enamel**?
4. What does most of **the inside of the tooth** consist of?
5. What name do we give to **the living part of the tooth**?
6. What is it that **holds the tooth in place**?
7. Which part of the tooth is **soft**?

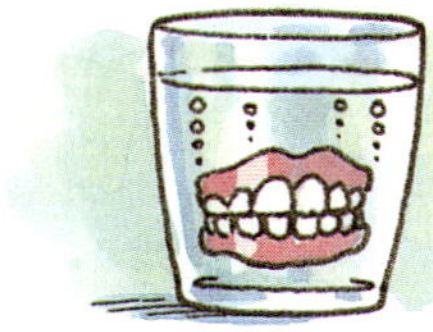

Teeth

Looking After Teeth

There are three things we should do to keep our teeth healthy. We should not eat too many sugary foods, especially between meals. We should brush our teeth at least twice a day, and we should visit the dentist regularly so that he or she can check our teeth for any signs of decay.

Paragraphs

A paragraph is a number of sentences about one main idea.

A

Read this paragraph about teeth.

1. What is the paragraph mainly about?
   a) visiting the dentist
   b) avoiding sugary foods
   c) keeping teeth healthy

How teeth go bad

1. In every mouth there are large numbers of bacteria. If teeth are not brushed these change food, especially sugar, into plaque.

2. Plaque is a sticky substance. It sticks to the surface of the tooth. When sugary foods are eaten the plaque reacts with the sugar to form an acid.

3. The acid soon begins to dissolve tooth enamel and may then eat its way through the enamel into the dentine. If the tooth is not filled the decay will spread through the dentine into the pulp.

4. When decay reaches the pulp, infection can occur. This may find its way to the root of the tooth and form an abcess. Sometimes the tooth has to be removed.

B

The four paragraphs on the left are about these topics:
a) decay
b) infection
c) bacteria
d) plaque
but not in that order.

Read the passage and match the number of each paragraph to its topic, like this:
1. c) bacteria

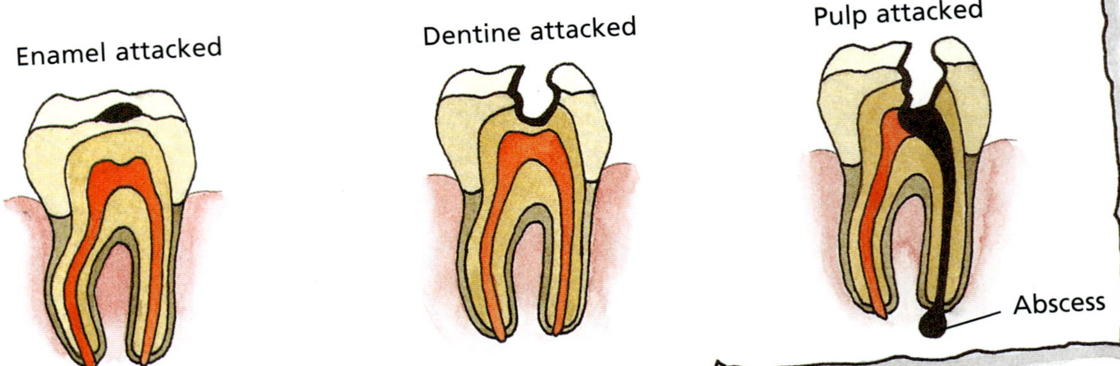

Flow diagrams

C

This flow diagram shows how teeth decay. The first three stages have been written in for you. Copy the diagram carefully and complete it by adding the remaining stages in the correct order.

Bacteria turn sugar into plaque.

▼

Plaque sticks to the teeth.

▼

Sugar reacts with plaque to make acid.

▼

?

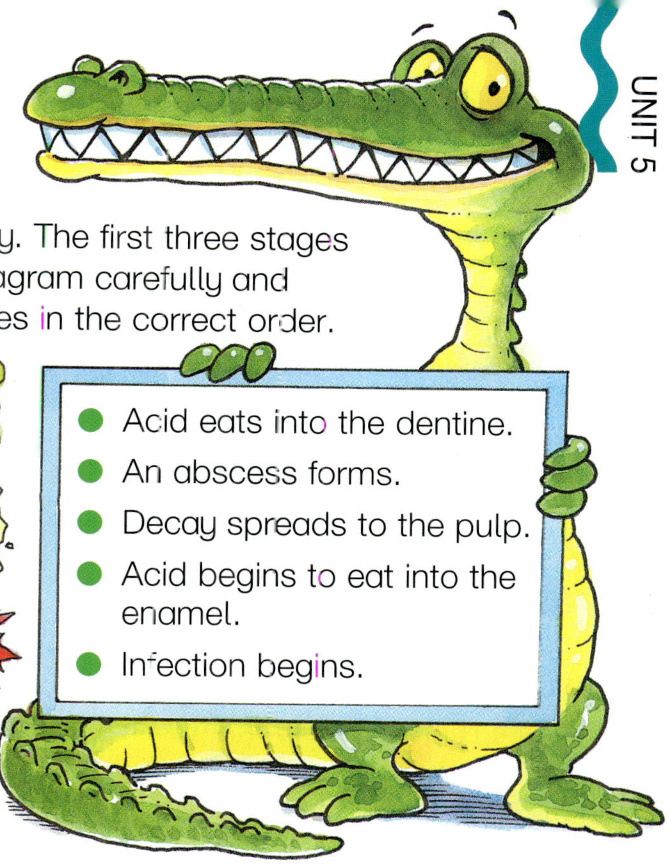

D How I brush my teeth

Make your own flow diagram to show how you brush your teeth. Begin with putting the toothpaste on the brush.

Using a glossary

A glossary is a list of explanations of specialist words, usually found at the back of a book.

There is a glossary at the back of this book. Can you find it?

E

Use this glossary to help you answer in complete sentences.

1. What sticky substance forms on **teeth**?
2. What does to **decay** mean?
3. What is **acid**?
4. What is an **abscess** caused by?
5. What do we use to see **bacteria**?
6. What is a **cavity**?
7. What is **infection**?

abscess	A painful swelling caused by infection.
acid	A liquid which burns skin and eats into metals.
bacteria	Living things which can only be seen with a microscope.
cavity	A small hole.
decay	To rot.
infection	A disease of some kind.
plaque	A soft sticky substance which forms on teeth.

Things That Go Bump in the Night

The Hairy Toe

Once there was a woman went out to
pick beans,
and she found a Hairy Toe.
She took the Hairy Toe home with her,
and that night, when she went to bed,
the wind began to moan and groan.
Away in the distance
She seemed to hear a voice crying,
'Where's my Hair-r-ry To-o-oe?
Who's got my Hair-r-ry To-o-oe?'

The woman scrooched down,
'way down under the covers,
and about that time
the wind appeared to hit the house,
smoosh,
and the old house creaked and cracked
like something was trying to get in.
The voice had come nearer,
almost at the door now,
and it said,
'Where's my Hair-r-ry To-o-oe?
Who's got my Hair-r-ry To-o-oe?'

The woman scrooched further down
under the covers
and pulled them tight around her head.

The wind growled around the house
like some big animal
and r-r-um-mbled
over the chimbley.
All at once she heard the door
cr-r-a-ack
and Something slipped in
and began to creep over the floor.

The floor went
cre-e-eak, cre-e-eak
at every step that thing took
towards her bed.
The woman could almost feel it
bending over her bed.
There in an awful voice it said:
'Where's my Hair-r-ry To-o-oe?
Who's got my Hair-r-ry To-o-oe?
YOU'VE GOT IT!'

Anon (Traditional American)

A About the poem

1. Did you enjoy the poem? Give a reason for your answer.
2. What do you think makes the poem so frightening?
3. Make a list of all the sounds in the poem.
4. Why do you think words such as 'cre-e-eak' are written like that?
5. What do you think 'scrooched' means? (Verse 2)
6. What do you think the owner of the Hairy Toe looks like? Draw a picture.
7. What do you think might happen next?

B Reading aloud

Ask your teacher if you can read the poem aloud with a partner. One of you may tell the story while the other is the mysterious voice. What do you think the voice might sound like?

C Sound words

1. What sound words can you think of to go with this picture?

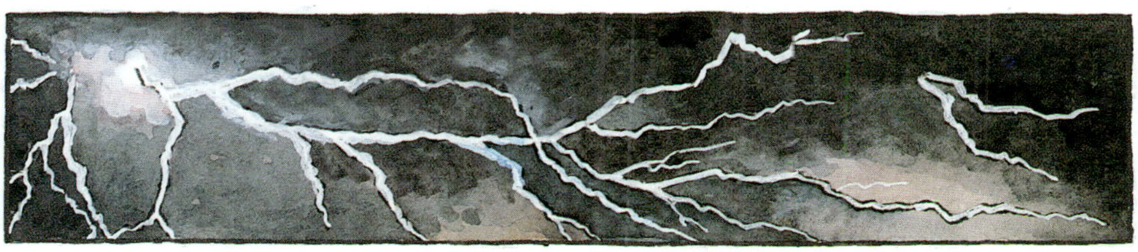

2. Draw pictures to show some of these sounds being made.

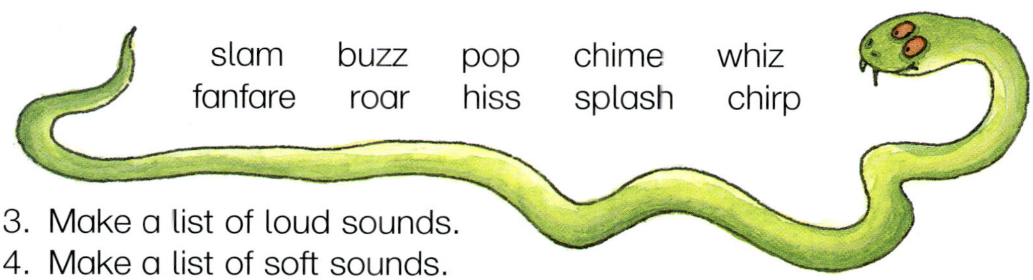

slam buzz pop chime whiz
fanfare roar hiss splash chirp

3. Make a list of loud sounds.
4. Make a list of soft sounds.
5. Choose two loud and two soft sounds. Use each one in a sentence to show its meaning.

D To write about

Think about a time when you were frightened by sounds in the dark. Write about it. Describe the sounds you heard and what made them seem so frightening. What happened in the end?

Things That Go Bump in the Night
Ghosts

The graveyard was dark. There was no sign of Simon. Martin looked quickly all around him and then carefully opened the iron gate. It creaked alarmingly. Martin held his breath and listened carefully. The graveyard remained still and quiet. He crept quietly towards the centre. The tall headstone of Joshua Barnes stood out darkly against the moonlit sky.

'Simon,' he called out nervously, 'Where are you?' Simon leapt out suddenly from behind the headstone.

'Here I am!' he laughed loudly. But his laugh did not last long. A sudden chill wind made the boys shiver. Then an echoing voice called out mysteriously,

'Who is standing on my grave?'

The words seemed to come from deep within the dark ground.

A Adjectives

Find the adjectives (describing words) in the passage above.
Make a list of them together with the nouns they describe.
Begin like this: 1. dark graveyard...

B Verbs and adverbs

Verbs are action words: crept, creaked, whispered, shouted.
Adverbs tell us more about verbs: crept **quietly**, creaked **alarmingly**, whispered **softly,** shouted **angrily**. Most adverbs end in **-ly**.

1. Find the adverbs in the passage above. Make a list of them together with the verbs they tell us more about.
   Begin like this: 1. looked quickly...
2. Find opposites to these adverbs:
   a) softly b) slowly c) happily d) carelessly
   e) noisily f) loosely g) heavily
3. Think of an adverb for each of these sentences.
   a) Jodie put her clothes away ________.
   b) He won the race ________.
   c) 'How dare you!' he shouted ________.
   d) 'I've lost my dog,' he said ________.
   e) He picked up the expensive ornament very ________.

Writing a ghost story

Ghost stories usually take place in an eerie (mysterious) setting. A **setting** is where and when a story takes place. The story on the opposite page takes place in a graveyard at night. Why do you think most ghost stories take place at night?

Choose one of these settings for your ghost story.

Your audience

- Whom are you writing your story for? A child or an adult? What sort of ghost might make them frightened?

Characters

- Whom will your story be about? Will your audience prefer to read about children, adults, or a mixture of both?

Setting

- The first paragraph of a ghost story is where you describe the eerie setting.
  Make a list of suitable **adjectives** to describe your setting and make your reader ready for strange and ghostly happenings.

Plot (the story)

- What will your characters do? What will they see and hear? What will happen when the ghost appears? Use lots of adjectives and adverbs to help your reader see clear pictures in his or her mind.
- How will your story end? Will the mystery be explained, or will it end like 'The Hairy Toe', leaving your reader wondering?

At Play

West Toys are the Best Toys!

Here are five of our top selling West Toys' products.

DISGUISER

The ace face changer!

Our best seller from the **Secrets** range of toys.
This set contains everything you need to disguise yourself. Mix and match for endless fun.
Contents: false beard, false moustache, four different pairs of glasses, two false noses, make up and face paints.

NEW!

WRIST COMMUNICATORS

Don't get left out! Buy the very latest walkie-talkie watches in our **Secrets** range. Two wrist watch-style communicators each with a flip-up lid, a mouth piece, speaker and pull-out flexible antenna. On/off volume control, on/off transmit key, morse key, power indicator, and a digital time display. Range up to 20m. Complete with batteries.

DESIGNER GEMS

Be the envy of your friends! Everything you need to create your own designer jewellery in a choice of five stunning styles. Contains 30 glass jewels, fixings, coloured baking clay, moulding mix, paints, varnish, glitter, brush, plastic jewellery shapes and a 24-page book of fabulous designs.

All West Toys come with a full guarantee of satisfaction, or your money back.
For a colour catalogue with full details on these and other West Toys' products send a large stamped addressed envelope to:
West Toys, Riverby Industrial Estate, Babbingdon, Dunshire, BA3 6DG.

A Reading for the main idea

1. What could you make with **Designer Gems**?
2. What kind of toy is **Space Buggy**?
3. What does the **Zoom Telescope** do?
4. What could you do with **Disguiser**?
5. What are **Wrist Communicators**?

B Reading for detail

1. How many pairs of **glasses** are supplied in **Disguiser**?
2. What is the **length** of the **Space Buggy**?
3. What is the **range** of the **Wrist Communicators**? What does that mean?
4. What is the **range** of the **Space Buggy**?
5. How many **glass jewels** does **Designer Gems** contain?
6. What extra item is supplied with the **Zoom Telescope**? What is it used for?
7. Which toys need **batteries**?
8. Which toy is supplied with a **book**?

C To think and write about

1. How many exclamation marks can you see in the West Toys' advertisement? Why do you think West Toys have used so many?
2. What does the advertisement say to persuade children to want:
   a) Designer Gems?
   b) Wrist Communicators?

D Writing letters

1. A relative asks you which of these toys you would like as a present. Write a letter saying what you have chosen and why you would like it.
2. Write a letter to West Toys asking for a colour catalogue.

At Play
Toys and Games

A Labelling a diagram

Look back at the description of the Wrist Communicators on page 28. Then match the labels to the diagram, like this: a) flip-up lid.

power indicator
flexible antenna
digital time display
morse key
mouth piece
on/off transmit key
flip-up lid
on/off volume control
speaker

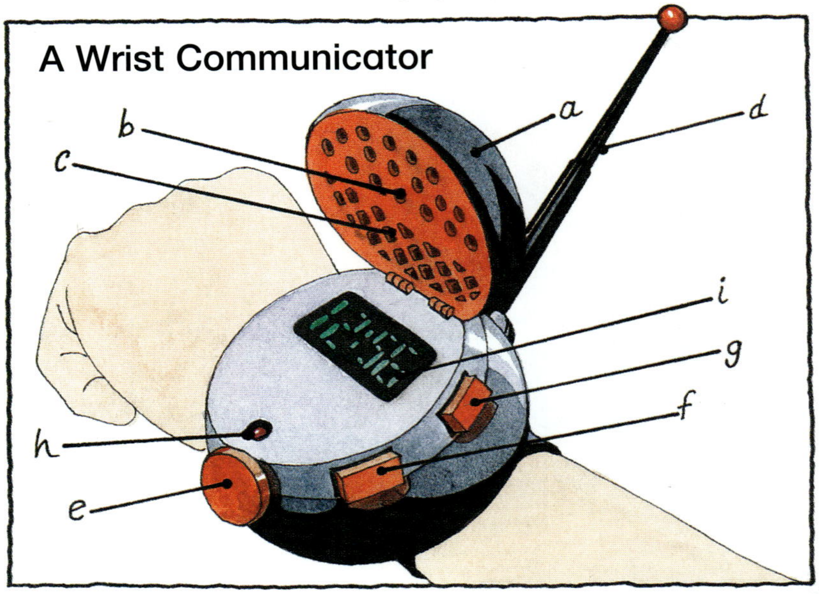

B Instructions

Make up your own instructions for the use of the Wrist Communicators. Begin: First open the flip-up lid...

C Design a toy

- Design a new toy for **Secrets**, West Toys' special range for detectives and secret agents.
- Draw a labelled diagram of the toy and explain how it works.
- Design a poster to advertise your toy.

Road Race

The instructions for the Road Race game on the opposite page have been lost. Write some new ones. Use these headings.

- **Number of players** (*how many people can play the game*)
- **Object of the game** (*what you need to do to win*)
- **Equipment** (*what you need to play the game*)
- **How to play** (*deciding who goes first, and what the rules are for playing*)

Start
Road Race
Broken bridge – go back 6 squares
Clear road – move on 3 squares
Run out of petrol – miss a turn
Good map reading – move on 4 squares
Road Works
Downhill run – move on 2 squares
Take wrong turning – go back 3 squares
Roadworks – miss a turn
Car running well – move on 3 squares
Traffic lights – miss a turn
Detour – go back 5 squares
Finish
Make good time – move on 4 squares
Diversion

Design a Pram

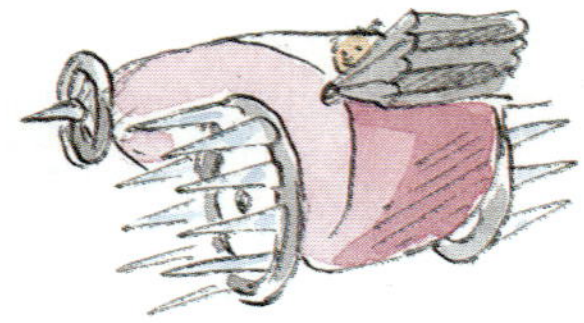

The teacher has asked the class to design a pram. The children have split themselves into two teams to see who can come up with the best design.

In Oliver Smart's team, there was a whisper argument raging about how the pram should be steered.

'Remote control,' insisted Douglas. 'What we need is a really good computer that stays in the house. Then whoever is controlling the pram just sits at home pressing the right buttons, or using a joystick, and the pram goes forwards or backwards, left or right.'

'We'll need a camera on the front of the pram, then. It sends live film of where the pram's going back to Mission Control.'

'The pram should be rocket-propelled,' said Ahmed. 'For fast speeds. And it should have retros for instant braking.'

'In that case we'll need it to be a lot more streamlined than the one in Philip's drawing,' said Stephen. 'Rub out the front, Philip, and draw it again, much more pointy.'

'What about the baby?' asked Roy.

'The baby will just have to be squashed up at the back,' said Laura. 'It's a bit safer up at the back, anyway, at high speeds.'

'We could give the baby a gamma ray gun,' suggested Douglas. 'Then it could pick off anyone who was sneaking up behind it.'

'Not "it",' said Jamie D. 'Babies aren't "it"!' He wasn't whispering any longer. He was talking quite loudly. 'Babies are "he" or "she". Little boys

or little girls. And they're far too young to be out on their own in a remote-controlled pram. Babies need looking after all the time. In fact they're happiest when they can hear a recording of their own mother's heartbeat close to them. They certainly shouldn't be encouraged to sit up and shoot people out of their prams.'

He looked up. Everyone else in the team was scowling at him, so he looked down again quickly.

'They wouldn't need to sit up and shoot people,' said Suzie, 'if you had sharp knives sticking out of the wheels.'

'Knives sticking out of the wheels! Brilliant!'

'That's a really good idea! You're a genius, Suzie! Do you want to join our team?'

'Yes please,' said Suzie. 'I wasn't getting on too well over there with that lot.'

From *Design a Pram* by Anne Fine

A Reading for detail

1. How will the pram be steered?
2. Why will it need a camera?
3. Why will it need 'retros'?
4. Why did Douglas want to give the baby a gamma ray gun?
5. What did Suzie suggest?
6. Why was she invited to join the team?
7. Who is drawing the team's design? How do you know?
8. Draw the pram the team designed. Label the parts.

B To think and write about

1. What do you think of the children's design for the pram? Give reasons for your answer.
2. What do you think the teacher will say when he sees it?

C Designing a pram

1. Make your own design for a pram. Draw it carefully and label the parts.
2. Write an explanation of how it works.

Design a Pram

Talking with Anne Fine

Anne Fine is the author of *Design a Pram* and many other popular books. Her book *Madame Doubtfire* was made into the film *Mrs. Doubtfire*. This is what she has to say about writing books.

When did you decide you wanted to write a book?
I didn't. I just wrote one. Trapped in the house by a snowstorm, and unable to get to the library, I started to write my first novel, *The Summer House Loon.*

Where do you get your ideas from?
Things I see, things I read, things I hear.

How long does it take to write a book?
For readers of ten and up, over a year. I think about it for quite a while. The writing itself takes nine months or so.

I write very slowly (in pencil, rubbing out constantly) then I type it up, recorrect, retype, recorrect, etc.

Why don't you use a word processor?
I think most writers have a natural speed, and the work can suffer if they go faster. The speed I go suits me.

What advice would you give a young writer?
Read, read, read. I believe the best practice for writing is not writing, but reading. My advice would be that of Robert Louis Stevenson: 'Read everything'.

Did you enjoy reading as a child?
Enormously. Totally. It was all I did.

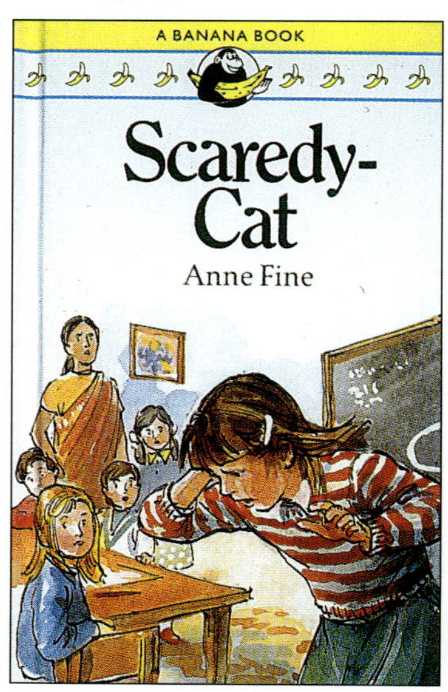

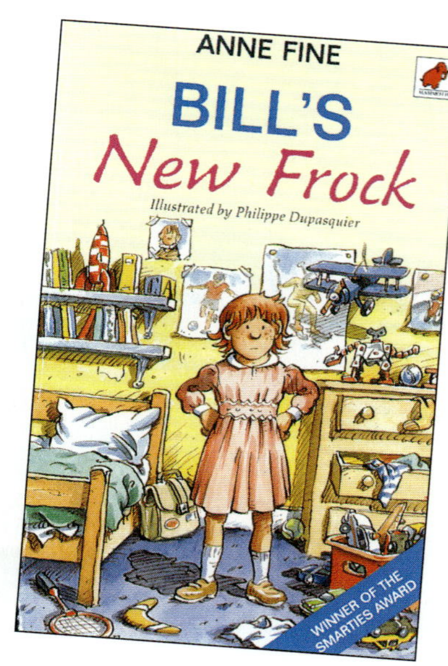

A About Anne Fine

1. What was Anne Fine's **first novel**?
2. How long does she take to **write a book**?
3. Where does she get her **ideas** from?
4. What did she enjoy doing most as a **child**?
5. Why doesn't she use a **word processor**?
6. What is her advice to **young writers**?

B Reading

'Read, read, read,' says Anne Fine. 'Read everything,' said Robert Louis Stevenson, author of *Treasure Island.*

Reading is a very important part of writing. Reading gives you ideas and shows how words are spelt and how they are arranged on the page. Here is a list of some of the ways in which reading will help you become a better writer. It is not written in any particular order. Rewrite the list in the order you think is most important to you.

- learning new words
- ways of beginning a story
- spelling
- ideas for setting
- ideas for characters
- ideas for stories
- how to set out your writing

C Writing to an author

Most people have a favourite book. Many people have a favourite author, whose new books they look forward to reading. Have you a favourite author?

Write a letter to an author whose work you have enjoyed.
Here are some things you might like to write about.

- Say why you enjoy this author's books, and which is your favourite.
- Ask questions about the author and how he or she writes.
- Send the author your own book review of one of his or her books.
- Send your own drawings, or a book cover design, for one of his or her books.

Look at the front of one of his or her books for the address of the publisher. Send your letter to the author c/o (care of) the publisher at that address. Enclose a large stamped addressed envelope for the author's reply.

The Library

It looks like any other building
When you pass it on the street,
Made of stone and glass and marble,
Made of iron and concrete.

But once inside you can ride
A camel or a train,
Visit Rome, Siam or Nome,
Feel a hurricane,
Meet a king, learn to sing,
How to bake a pie,
Go to sea, plant a tree,
Find how airplanes fly,
Train a horse, and of course
Have all the dogs you'd like,
See the moon, a sandy dune,
Or catch a whopping pike.
Everything that books can bring
You'll find inside those walls.
A world is there for you to share
When adventure calls.

You cannot tell its magic
By the way the building looks,
But there's wonderment within it,
The wonderment of books.

Barbara A. Huff

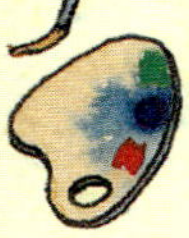

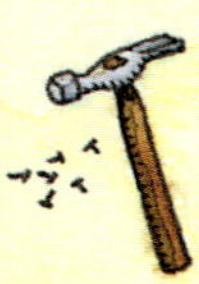

About the poem

1. Why is it hard to tell that a library has magic inside it?
2. Where does a library keep its magic?
3. Name three things the poem says a library can help you learn to do.
4. Name three places you can visit there.
5. Name two things you can ride on.
6. Explain how a library might let you 'have all the dogs you'd like'.

Books

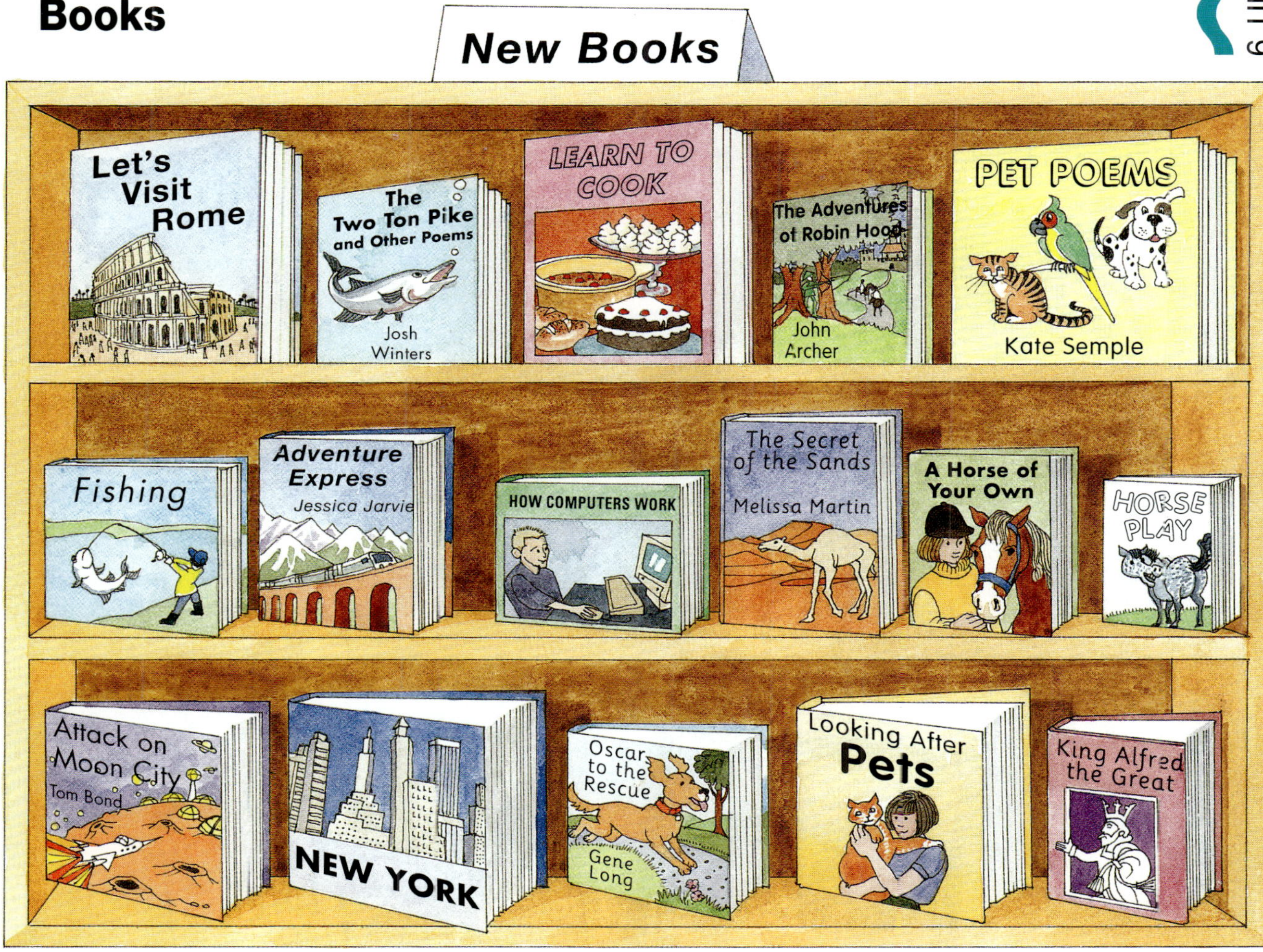

A Sorting books

This is the New Books display shelf in a library. The books are displayed here for two weeks before being placed on the main book shelves. The story books will then go on the fiction shelves and the poetry books on the poetry shelf. The books about real things and real people will go on the non-fiction shelves. Make separate lists of:

a) the fiction books;
b) the poetry books;
c) the non-fiction books.

B Fiction Books

Fiction books are arranged in alphabetical order of the author's last name. Make an alphabetical list of all the fiction books like this:

Shelf	Author	Title
A	Archer, John	The Adventures of Robin Hood

C Non-fiction books

Write the titles of books which tell us about:

a) places;
b) people;
c) how to do things;
d) how things work.

The Library
A Book and Its Cover

Book covers are carefully designed to give the reader a fair idea of what a book is about. Look at these covers.

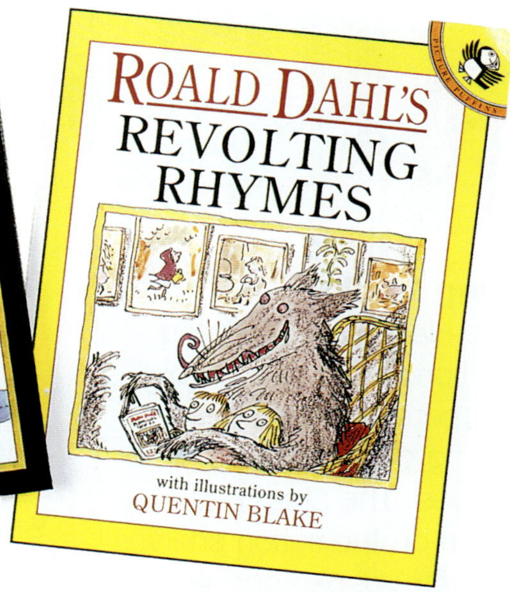

A Looking at covers

1. Which are stories about animals?
2. Which book will tell you about real animals?
3. Which is a book of verse?
4. Which books might make you laugh?
5. Choose one of the above books which you have not read. Write a few lines saying what you think it might be about. What clues helped you to decide?

B Matching

Match these extracts to the book covers.
First write the number of the extract and then the book's title.

1 Stretched across the upper part of the doorway was a big spider's web, and hanging from the top of the web, head down, was a large grey spider.

2 'Oh Mirror Mirror on the wall,
Who is the fairest of them all?'
The Mirror answered every time,
'Oh Madam, you're the Queen sublime.
You are the only one to charm us,
Queen, you are the cat's pyjamas.'

3 Woodlands contain a wealth of animal- and plant-life which needs to be carefully protected if the balance of nature within woodlands is not to be upset. You can help by not damaging trees and other plants, and by not disturbing birds and other animals unnecessarily.

4 He grabbed the toothpaste carton and studied the writing. Just as he had thought! It did say, 'VENGER'S PURPLE SPECKLED TRUTHPASTE', and the small print underneath read: 'Guaranteed to make you tell the truth for twenty-four hours after use'.

5 There he lay, a vast red-golden dragon, fast asleep; a thrumming came from his jaws and nostrils, and wisps of smoke, but his fires were low in slumber.

C Looking for answers

Look in the extracts above for the answers to these questions.

1. How can you help protect life in **woodlands**?
2. What colour is the sleeping **dragon**?
3. For how long does **Venger's Truthpaste** work?
4. Where was the **spider** hanging from?
5. Who is **'the only one to charm us'**?

D Writing a story

Read extract 4 again. Suppose you had a tube of Venger's Truthpaste. Who would you give it to? What might happen? Write a story about it.

Finding Out

Where do we find the answers?

a What does twilight mean?

b ?

c What is my friend's telephone number?

d What do crocodiles eat?

e Who was the tallest man? How tall was he?

f Will it rain today?

g Which five words mean the same as 'laugh'?

h Where can I find a plumber?

A

1. Say where you think the answers may be found.
   Begin: a) a dictionary...
2. Find the answers to as many of the questions as you can.

B

1. Write five questions of your own. Underline the key words.
2. For each one say where you think you may find the answers.
3. Look for the answers.

Non-fiction books

The non-fiction books in a library are grouped under topics. Look at this topic web.

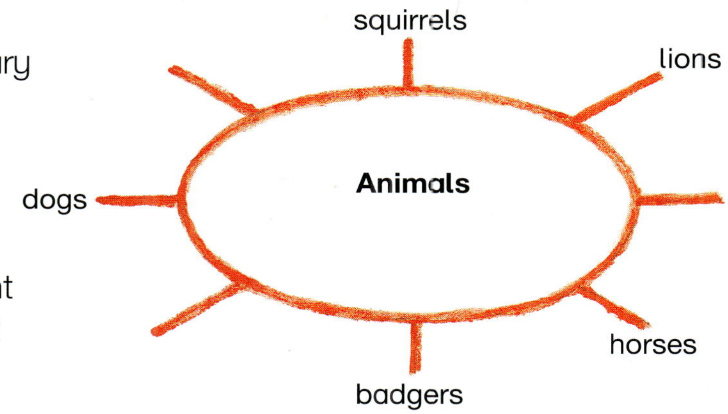

The main topic is animals. The sub-topics are the different kinds of animals. Books about all these would be grouped together on the Animals shelf.

1. Copy the topic web above into your book. Think of three more animals to complete it.
2. Copy these topic webs into your book. Choose sub-topics from the word bank to complete them.

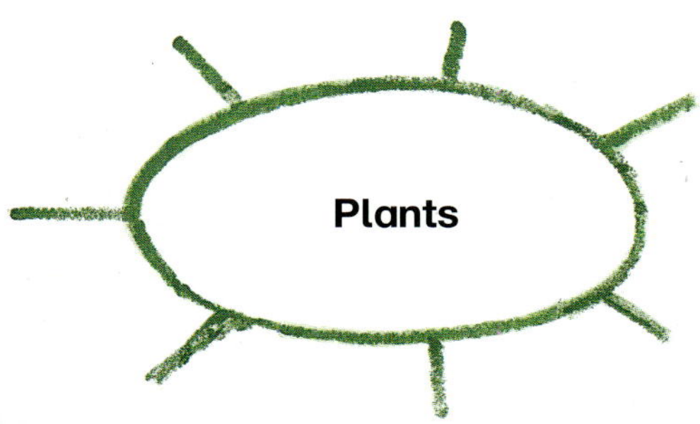

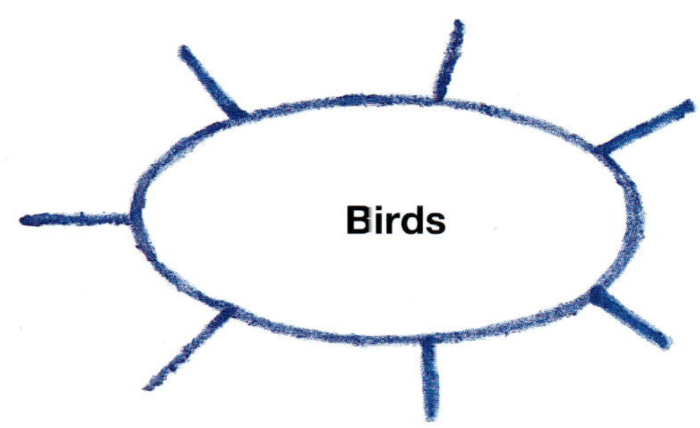

hawk primrose robin chaffinch ivy sparrow holly
tulip eagle parrot orchid magpie marigold moss

3. Make topic webs of your own for these.
   a) Sports b) Famous People
4. Copy each question below. Underline the key words. Write the topic heading to look for in the library.
   a) What colour is a raven?
      Begin: What <u>colour</u> is a <u>raven</u>? Topic: Birds...
   b) What is the home of a badger?
   c) What colour is a honeysuckle flower?
   d) How many players are there in a hockey team?
   e) Who was Abraham Lincoln?
   f) Where do penguins live?
   g) What is a baby owl called?
   h) Is an oak tree deciduous?
5. Look for the answers to the above questions.

Finding Out
Reporting

A

Read the newspaper report below.
Look for the answers to these questions.

1. **What** special event took place?
2. **Where** did it happen?
3. **When** did it happen?
4. **Whom** did Tiffany go to see?
5. **Why** did she go there?

The Newtown Messenger ◆ 3rd November

Pop star visits local school

A dream came true today for local school children, when American pop superstar Tiffany Temple called in to meet them. It all began when 10-year old Gemma Winters wrote a letter to her idol as part of an English lesson at Fairfield Junior School. 'I asked her to come and see us if she was ever in town,' said an excited Gemma this afternoon. 'I never expected she would!'

Tiffany took time off her busy concert tour to spend an hour at the school, answering questions about the pop business and signing autographs. 'My great grandfather used to live in this area before he emigrated to America,' she said. 'I just couldn't resist taking the opportunity to see the old place and meet Gemma and her friends.' Mrs. Wendy Green, the head teacher, was delighted at the visit. 'Tiffany was a wonderful guest. I hope she finds time to pay us another visit soon.' The children of Fairfield Junior couldn't agree more.

B

Read carefully the words of Gemma, Tiffany and Mrs. Green. Write the questions you think the reporter asked them.

Writing a report

You are a newspaper reporter at the scene of an accident. Look closely at the picture.

1. Copy and complete the notes.
2. Write down any questions you would like to ask about the accident.
3. Make up answers for your questions.
4. Write a full report using your notes.
5. Think up a good headline for your story.

The First Writing

1 Prehistoric people had not developed writing. Instead they painted picture stories of hunting on the walls of their caves. They made paint by crushing coloured rock and mixing it with grease, egg white, resin or water. This made a paste-powder of yellow, red, brown or black. They painted with their fingers, or with a brush made from hair, feathers, fur or pieces of bark tied together.

2 About 5000 years ago the people of Sumeria were the first to develop pictures into writing. They needed to keep records of the number of farm animals they owned or objects they made. At first they scratched their picture words, or pictograms, on stone or metal, but later they drew them on tablets of wet clay, using a piece of bone, wood or reed. The tablets were then dried in the sun, or baked in an oven.

3 They soon found that it was difficult to draw circles or curves without smudging the wet clay. They changed the picture language so that it used only straight lines. At the same time they found it easier to draw the sign pictures sideways on. The marks they pressed into the clay were wedge-shaped, and we now call this cuneiform. The name comes from two Latin words: *cuneus* (wedge) and *forma* (shape).

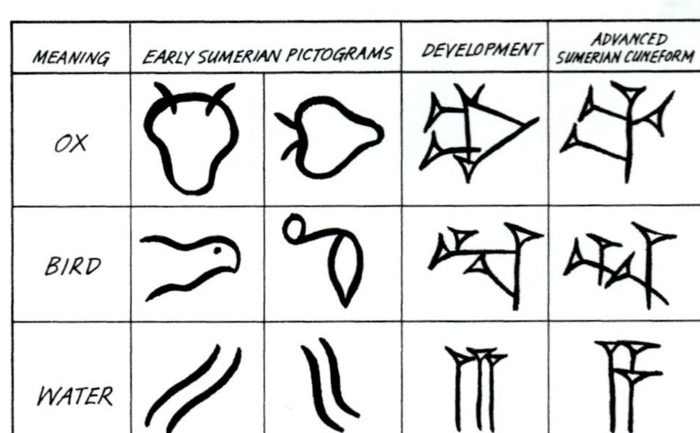

A The main idea

1. What is the main idea of the passage? Only one of these sentences tells us what the main idea really is.
   a) Prehistoric people painted with their fingers.
   b) The first writing developed from pictures.
   c) Sumerian tablets were dried in the sun.

2. What is the main idea of paragraph 1?
   a) Prehistoric people made paint from powdered rock.
   b) Prehistoric people painted with their fingers or simple brushes.
   c) Prehistoric people painted picture stories.

3. What is the main idea of paragraph 2?
   a) Sumerians were the first to develop pictures into writing.
   b) Sumerians scratched their first pictures on stone or metal.
   c) The clay tablets were dried in the sun, or baked in an oven.

4. What is the main idea of paragraph 3?
   a) Wet clay is easily smudged.
   b) The pictures changed into cuneiform writing.
   c) Cuneiform means wedge-shaped.

B Words and pictures

1. Make your own word pictures for these.

a) tree	b) horse	c) sun	d) moon	e) cloud
f) hill	g) river	h) forest	i) day	j) night

2.  +  = 

star + fish = starfish

Which words do these pictures make?

a)  +  b) 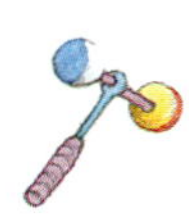 +  c)  + 

3. Make your own word pictures for these.
   a) toadstool b) cupboard c) windmill d) honeycomb e) horseshoe

4. Continue this story using pictures for as many words as you can.

Once upon a  a  went into the  to 

The First Writing
Hieroglyphics

The people of Egypt developed a form of picture writing we now call hieroglyphics. It began, like Sumerian cuneiform, with pictures standing for objects. Gradually it became like an alphabet, with pictures standing for sounds. This made writing much easier, because instead of needing pictures for thousands of objects, the Egyptians could now spell their words with just a few hieroglyphs. Some of the letters in our alphabet had no hieroglyphic equivalent.

A	**B**	**D**	**F**	**G**	**H**	**I**	**J**	**K**	**L**
Vulture	Leg	Hand	Viper	Stand	Rope	Reed	Serpent	Basket	Lion

			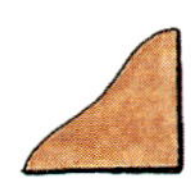		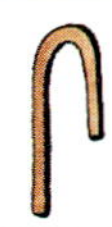			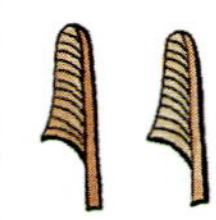	
M	**N**	**P**	**Q**	**R**	**S**	**T**	**W**	**Y**	**Z**
Owl	Water	Stool	Hill	Mouth	Cloth	Loaf	Chick	Reeds	Bolt

Reading hieroglyphics is difficult because there are no spaces between words.

ITISNOTEASYTOREADIFTHEREARENOSPACESBETWEENWORDS

The missing letters, especially the vowels E, O and U, make it even more difficult to read. In hieroglyphics a sentence such as

PLEASE HELP ME UNLOCK THE DOOR would be written as

PLASHLPMNLKTHDR

To make it even more difficult there were no punctuation marks, such as full stops or question marks, so one sentence would run into another.

The Ancient Egyptians wrote on papyrus, which was made from the stem of the papyrus plant. The stem was cut into strips and beaten until wafer thin. The beating released a sap which allowed the strips to be glued together, making a kind of paper. The Egyptians used pens made from reeds. They dipped these in ink, which was usually red or black. They also carved hieroglyphics on the walls of temples. The word hieroglyphics comes from two Greek words which mean 'sacred' and 'carving'.

A About hieroglyphics

Copy each question and underline the key words. Then look for the answers.

1. What is Egyptian picture writing called?
   Begin like this: What is <u>Egyptian picture writing</u> called?
2. How did it become like an alphabet?
3. Why did that make writing much easier?
4. Which of our letters have no hieroglyphic equivalents?
5. List three things that make it difficult to read hieroglyphics.
6. What is papyrus made from?
7. How is it made into a kind of paper?
8. What were Egyptian pens made from?
9. Where were hieroglyphics carved?
10. Why do you think it was easier for the Egyptians to write in pictures than it was for the Sumerians?

B Writing

1. Make up your own hieroglyphs for the letters missing from our alphabet.
2. Write your name and those of your friends in hieroglyphics.
3. Write this sentence without spaces between words and without E, O or U:

   READING HIEROGLYPHICS ON PAPYRUS IS NOT EASY
4. Rewrite the same sentence in hieroglyphics.
5. Make up hieroglyphs for a full stop, question mark and exclamation mark.
6. Write a message to a friend using Egyptian hieroglyphs.

A Fairy Story

A About the picture

1. What time of year is it?
   How do you know?
2. Who might the children be?
3. Why are they are going to the cottage?
4. Who do you think lives in the cottage?
5. How do the children feel as they push open the door?
   What are they thinking?
6. What do the children see and hear as they go in?
7. What might happen next?

B Describing

1. Describe the children.
   How old are they? How are they dressed? What are they carrying?
2. Describe the cottage.
   Look at the windows, the door, the chimney and the roof.
   What can you see outside the cottage?

C Writing a fairy story

Use your answers to help you write a fairy story. Include your descriptions.

Cinderella

Read the beginnings of these different versions of the Cinderella story.

Once upon a time there lived a young girl called Cinderella whose mother died. Her father married a cruel widow with two daughters of her own. They couldn't bear Cinderella and treated her very badly indeed.

1

There was once a young woman named Cinderella who had a cruel stepmother, two cruel and ugly stepsisters, and a father who was not around much.

One day the postman arrived with an invitation to the Royal Ball. The stepmother and the sisters got dressed in their finery and departed almost at once, leaving Cinderella alone.

From *The Jolly Postman* by Janet and Allan Ahlberg

2

I guess you think you know this story.
You don't. The real one's much more gory.
The phoney one, the one that you know,
Was cooked up years and years ago,
And made to sound all soft and sappy
Just to keep the children happy.
Mind you they got the first bit right,
The bit where in the dead of night,
The Ugly Sisters, jewels and all,
Departed for the Palace Ball,
While darling little Cinderella
Was locked up in a slimy cellar,
Where rats who wanted things to eat,
Began to nibble at her feet.

From *Revolting Rhymes* by Roald Dahl

3

A About the stories

1. Which version is closest to the Cinderella you know best?
2. Which is in verse? How can you tell?
3. Which do you think is the most likely to end 'they all lived happily ever after'? What makes you think so?
4. Which is likely to be very different from the story we all know well? What makes you think so?
5. Which version do you prefer? Give a reason for your answer.

B New for old

Make up a new version of your favourite fairy story. Change what happens in the story, keeping it similar, but different. Make the main character behave in a new way. Give the story a different ending.

A Fairy Story

Favourite Fairy Stories

A Favourites

1. Which is your favourite fairy story? Give a reason for your answer.
2. Which is your least favourite fairy story? Give as many reasons as you can.

B Conducting a survey

1. **Finding out**
   Ask your friends and adults which fairy stories they like best, and which they like least.
2. **Recording**
   Record the answers of children and adults separately.
3. **Presenting the results**
   How many ways of presenting your results can you think of?

I hereby announce the results of the royal survey on the favourite fairy stories of the good people of this fair land

C

1. Which is the children's favourite fairy story?
2. How many votes did it get?
3. How many children like Little Red Riding Hood best?
4. How many children like Goldilocks best?
5. How many stories were chosen?
6. How many children were asked about their favourite?
7. Present the results as a top five.

Green Bean Cottage
Tuesday

Dear Friend,

I hope you are keeping well. Mother sends her love.

You're not going to believe this. I sold our cow for some magic beans yesterday. This morning I looked out of the window and saw a beanstalk growing up through the clouds! I want to climb up it to see where it goes, but mother says it looks dangerous.

What shall I do? Would you like to come with me?

Please write soon and let me know.

Love and best wishes,
Jack

D

1. Write a reply to Jack's letter, agreeing to go with him.
2. Write a story about your adventures together.

Maps

A About the map

1. In which road is the school?
2. What important building is on East Street?
3. What is opposite the hospital?
4. In which road is the garage?
5. On which corner is the factory?

B Compass directions

What building is:

a) north of the park?
b) south of the park?
c) east of the school?
d) south of the mosque?
e) north of the supermarket?
f) west of the park?

C Directions chart

1. This chart shows the directions from the park of two important places. Copy the chart carefully and complete it by adding the missing places.

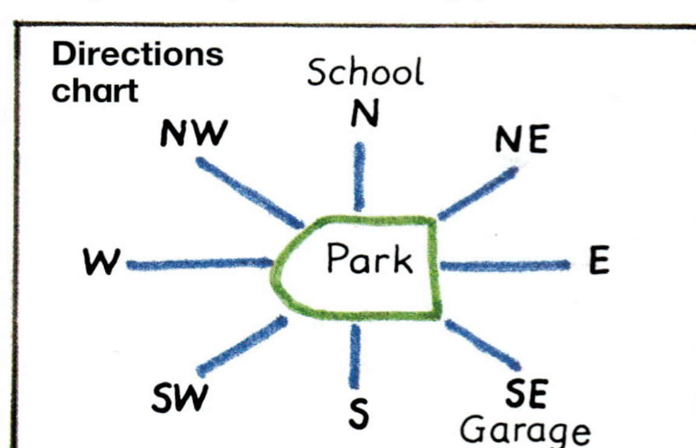

2. Make a similar chart for the important places near your school. You will need a compass to find the eight directions.

Map squares

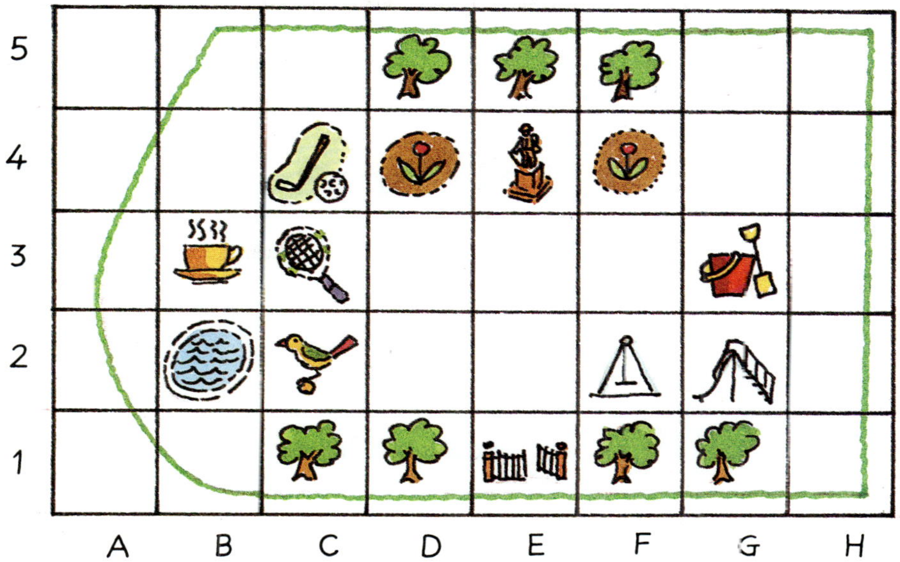

Look at this map of the park. The squares are called grid squares. They help you find places on the map.

Look for the swings. Their grid square is in column F and row 2. We say the swings are in square F2.

1. What is in each of these grid squares?
   a) G3 b) B2 c) E4
   d) D5 e) C4 f) G2
2. What are the grid squares for these?
   a) tennis court b) café
   c) the gates d) flower bed
   e) aviary

A Key

Every map needs a key. A key is a chart showing what the map symbols stand for.

This is the key to the map of the park. Copy it carefully in your book and fill in the missing boxes.

Symbol	Meaning	Square
	café	B3

		F5

	tennis court	
		E4
	flower bed	

		G3

	slide	
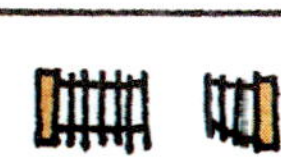		

Maps
Pirate Gold

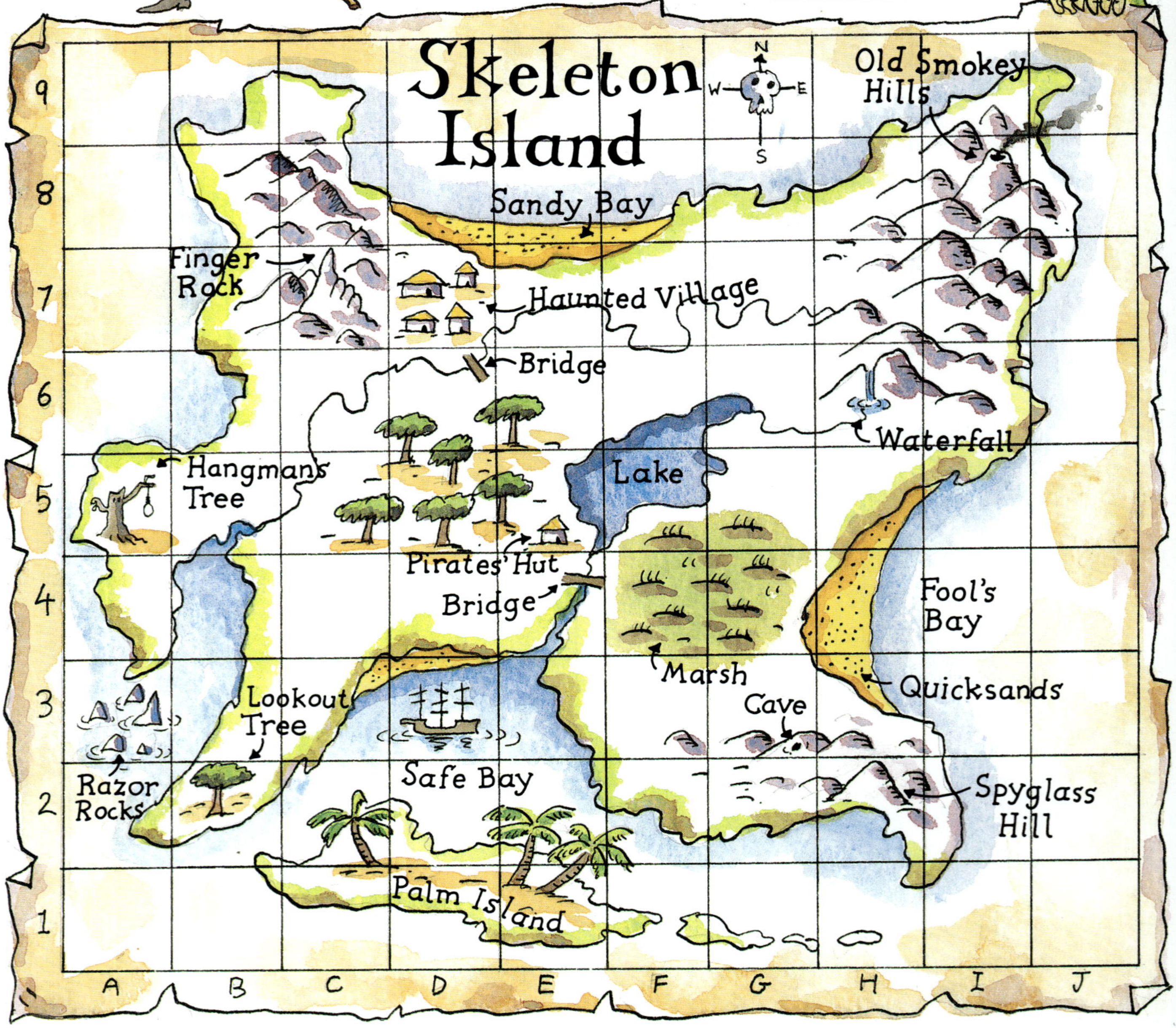

A About the map

1. Where did One-eyed Jack anchor his ship?
2. Where are the quicksands?
3. What is the name of the volcano?
4. Where is the pirates' hut?
5. What is the name of the rock near the haunted village?
6. In which direction is the marsh from the lake?
7. In which direction is Hangman's Tree from the pirates' hut?
8. What lies to the south of Safe Bay?

One-eyed Jack's Journal

We anchored in Safe Bay. Then we took a small boat north and landed on a sandy beach. We walked east along the sands and then north, past the wooden bridge. We spent the night at our old hut.

The following morning we set off again, keeping to the shore of the lake. We followed the river as far as the waterfall. There, in a cave behind the rushing waters, I buried my treasure.

B Grid squares

1. Make a list of the grid squares One-eyed Jack travelled through from his ship to the treasure cave. Begin like this: D3, D4, ...

2. One-eyed Jack did not go straight back to the hut. Instead he went on another journey. These are the squares he travelled through.
   H7, G7, F7, E7, D7, C7, D7, D6, D5, E5

Imagine you are the pirate. Continue your journal, saying where you went and what you did there.

3. Write the grid squares you would travel through to get from the hut to:
   a) Spyglass Hill
   b) Hangman's Tree
   c) Lookout Tree

C Place names

The island has some strange place names. Write a sentence for each of these places, saying why they were so named.

a) Finger Rock
b) Razor Rocks
c) Old Smokey Hills
d) Lookout Tree
e) Palm Island
f) Safe Bay
g) Fool's Bay
h) Haunted Village
i) Spyglass Hill
j) Skeleton Island

Word Play

Have you ever seen?

Have you ever seen
a blue tadpole
Have you ever seen
a spoilt-brat toad

Have you ever seen
a walking fish
Have you ever seen
a grunting chick

Have you ever seen
a singing spider
Have you ever seen
a dancing tiger

Have you ever seen
a monkey swimming
Have you ever seen
a turtle grinning

Have you ever?

Grace Nichols

A About the poem

1. What pictures does the poem make in your mind? Make a list of them.
2. How does the poem make you feel? Give a reason for your answer.
3. Does the poem rhyme?
4. Tap out the rhythm of the poem. Is it a regular rhythm?

B Writing a poem

Write your own 'Have you ever seen?' poem. Use Grace Nichol's poem as a model, but make up your own word pictures for lines 2 and 4 in each verse.

Planning

Make a list of animals you could include in your poem. Write down ideas for funny things you would never see them doing.

Presentation

When you have finished your poem, copy it out in your best handwriting. Decorate it with amusing pictures.

More ideas for poems

A Disappearing words

dancing tiger
ancing tiger
ncing tiger
cing tiger
ing tiger
ng tiger
g tiger
tiger
iger
ger
er
r

1. Try this with one of the word pictures from your 'Have you ever seen?' poem.
2. Read your poem aloud.

B Alphabet poems

In an alphabet poem the first line begins with A, the second with B and so on.
Write two alphabet poems of your own like these.
Try to write a line for each letter of the alphabet.

Things I like

Aunty Jane's cakes
Butterflies with colourful wings
Cuddly toys
Drawing pictures
Easter eggs with cream inside

Things I hate

Arguing with my sister
Being kept in
Cry babies
Drinking cold tea
Empty purses
Fighting

C Acrostics

In an acrostic the first letters of the lines spell out the subject of the poem.

Softly falling,
New and clean,
Outside my
Window.

Fishes of gold
In clear, cold water,
Silently swimming in a
House of glass.

Write an acrostic poem of your own.

Word Play

I Don't Believe It!

True Story

This morning I jumped on my horse
And went for a ride,
And some wild outlaws chased me
And they shot me in the side.
So I crawled into a wildcat's cave
To find a place to hide,
But some pirates found me sleeping there,
And soon they had me tied
To a pole and built a fire
Under me – I almost cried
Till a mermaid came and cut me loose
And begged to be my bride,
So I said I'd come back Wednesday
But I must admit I lied.
Then I ran into a jungle swamp
But I forgot my guide
And I stepped into some quicksand,
And no matter how I tried
I couldn't get out, until I met
A water snake named Clyde,
Who pulled me to some cannibals
Who planned to have me fried.
But an eagle came and swooped me up
And through the air we flied,
But he dropped me in a boiling lake
A thousand miles wide.
And you'll never guess what I did then –
I DIED.

Shel Silverstein

A About the poem

1. Do you think this story is true? Give a reason for your answer.
2. Did you enjoy the poem? Why?
3. Which part do you think is the most amusing? Why?
4. Why do you think the poet wrote 'And through the air we flied'?
5. Draw a picture of one of the adventures in the poem.

B Writing

Write your own story of fantastic adventures which no one could possibly believe.

A most peculiar pet

A Invent a pet

Make up an imaginary animal to keep as a pet. Draw a picture of it. Give your pet a name.

B Write about your pet

Plan

Paragraph 1:

- what your pet is called
- what it looks like
- what it eats
- where it sleeps
- the noise it makes
- how it moves

Paragraph 2:

- how it behaves when it is:

  hungry
  angry
  happy
  frightened
  cold
  tired

Paragraph 3:

- its worst habit
- its best habit
- why you like it as a pet

C Taking care of your pet

Write full instructions on how to take care of your pet. Include such things as:
how to feed it;
how to take it for a walk;
how to put it to bed;
how to reward it for good behaviour.
Make a list of things it must not be allowed to do. Give your reasons.

D Taking your pet to school

Write the story of what happened when you took your pet to school.

Weather

Christopher Robin lived at the very top of the Forest. It rained, and it rained, and it rained, but the water couldn't come up to his house. It was rather jolly to look into the valleys and see the water all round him, but it rained so hard that he stayed indoors most of the time, and thought about things. Every morning he went out with his umbrella and put a stick in the place where the water came up to, and every next morning he went out and couldn't see his stick any more, so he put another stick in the place where the water came up to, and then he walked home again, and each morning he had a shorter walk to walk than he had had the morning before. On the morning of the fifth day he saw the water all round him, and he knew that for the first time in his life he was on a real island. Which was very exciting.

It was on this morning that Owl came flying over the water to say 'How do you do?' to his friend Christopher Robin.

'I say, Owl,' said Christopher Robin, 'isn't this fun? I'm on an island.'

The atmospheric conditions have been very unfavourable lately,' said Owl.

'The what?'

'It has been raining,' explained Owl.

'Yes,' said Christopher Robin. 'It has.'

'The flood-level has reached an unprecedented height.'

'The who?'

'There's a lot of water about,' explained Owl.

From *Winnie-the-Pooh* by A. A. Milne

A About the story

1. Why did Christopher Robin think the water couldn't come up to his house?
2. What did Christopher Robin do every morning?
3. How did he know the water was rising?
4. Explain why his walk was shorter each day.
5. How did he feel when he saw water all around him?
6. What did Owl really mean when he said, 'The atmospheric conditions have been very unfavourable lately'?

Sun and rain

B Why?

Read carefully what each person is saying. Then write a sentence explaining why they are saying it.
Begin like this: 1. The boy says rain is boring because...

C Fact and opinion

Some of what these people are saying is **fact**. This means that what they are saying is **true**.
Others are giving their own **opinions**. They are saying what they **think**, but other people may disagree.

1. Make a list of the facts.
2. Make a list of the opinions.

D Good and bad points

1. Make a list of all the good points you can think of for rain.
2. Make a second list of its bad points.
3. Make similar lists of good and bad points for hot weather.

E Rain

Use your lists on rain to write a few sentences on its good points, and a few more on its bad points.

Weather

The Wind

The Wind

I can get through a doorway without any key,
And strip the leaves from the great oak tree.

I can drive storm-clouds and shake tall towers,
Or steal through a garden and not wake the flowers.

Seas I can move and ships I can sink;
I can carry a house-top or the scent of a pink.

When I am angry I can rave and riot;
And when I am spent, I lie quiet as quiet.

James Reeves

A About the poem

1. Explain how the wind 'can get through a doorway without any key'.
2. What does 'I can carry a house-top' mean?
3. What is 'the scent of a pink'?
4. Write a line from the poem in which the wind is gentle.
5. Write the line in which the wind is most dangerous.
6. Which is your favourite line? Copy it in your best writing and draw a picture of it.

B Wind strength

Look carefully at the pictures below. Use the Beaufort Wind Scale to find the wind strength for each picture. The first one has been done for you.

1. Strength 0, calm.

The Beaufort Wind Scale

The Beaufort Wind Scale shows winds in order of strength, with calm winds at the top and very strong winds at the bottom. The lightest is strength 0, which means calm. The strongest is strength 12, which is a hurricane.

Wind strength	Description	Wind speed in kms per hour	Effects that can be seen
0	calm	below 1	smoke rises straight up
1	light air	1–5	smoke drifts slightly
2	light breeze	6–11	leaves rustle, wind felt on face, wind vanes move
3	gentle breeze	12–19	leaves and small twigs move
4	moderate breeze	20–28	dust and loose papers blow about, flags flap, small branches sway
5	fresh breeze	29–38	small trees sway
6	strong breeze	39–49	large branches sway, telephone wires whistle, umbrellas difficult to use
7	moderate gale	50–61	trees sway, hard to walk against the wind
8	fresh gale	62–74	twigs break off trees, very hard to walk into wind
9	strong gale	75–88	slight damage to houses, large branches break off trees
10	storm	89–102	trees uprooted, serious damage to houses
11	violent storm	103–117	houses badly damaged
12	hurricane	118+	disaster, terrible damage

C About the Beaufort Wind Scale

1. Sort these into order of strength, lightest wind first: gale, breeze, hurricane, storm.
2. What is the wind strength of:
   a) a strong gale?
   b) a fresh breeze?
   c) a violent storm?
   d) a moderate gale?
3. What is the wind speed of:
   a) a light breeze?
   b) a moderate breeze?
   c) calm?
   d) a hurricane?
4. What happens in:
   a) light air?
   b) a gentle breeze?
   c) a fresh gale?
   d) a strong breeze?

D Writing

Use the Beaufort Scale to describe what happens as the wind increases from strength 0 to strength 10.

Television

Now the TV screen showed the racecourse crowds. The cameras went from person to person.

'Look!' Shani gasped. 'That was me! I just saw me! I can't believe it!'

'Impossible,' Ben said, and reached for the Blopper.

Before he could use it, the telly changed channels all by itself!

'I don't understand these humans,' the telly said to itself. 'But I think... if I try... I can show these two something they will really like!'

The screen showed a nature programme. A man and a woman, both in sweaters and gumboots, talked about field mice. The camera moved in to show a close-up of a pretty little mouse with bright eyes and twinkling whiskers.

The mouse was held cupped in a hand. Not the man's hand. Or the woman's. The hand of a young girl, a brown hand...

And a young girl's voice said, 'There, now! Who's a lovely mouse? Who's a little darling?'

'Me! squeaked Shani. 'That's me!'

Again Ben said, 'Impossible!' Then he said, 'Where am I?'

'Oh, somewhere in the background,' Shani said. She was staring at the screen, nodding her head and smiling to encourage the telly to show more of her.

'Well, she's pleased with me!' the TV said to itself. 'Though I can't think why. What's so special about being just a voice and a picture in a box?'

From *The Telly is Watching You* by Nicholas Fisk

A About the passage

1. What is unusual about Shani's TV?
2. What does Ben think about Shani on the screen?
3. What do you think the Blopper is?
4. How can you tell the TV is trying to please the children?
5. How does Shani try to encourage the TV to show more of her?
6. What do you think might happen next?
7. Give the passage a suitable title.

B To write about

Suppose your TV could put you on the screen? What would you like to see yourself doing? What would your family and friends think about it all?

TV programmes

BBC 1

3.30 Dodge and Bodgit
Part 4: We'll have it fixed in no time!
More fun with the dodgy repair men.

3.55 Cartoon Time

4.15 Bill's New Frock
Part 3: Bill gets into a fight with Rohan.

4.45 The Book Tree
Danni Douglas takes a look at the latest children's books.

5.00 Action Zone
TV's top children's magazine programme. Today's specials: stalactites, stetsons, stopwatches and stir fry!

5.35 Brewster's Cove
First episode in a brand new series. The peace of Brewster's Cove is shattered when a mysterious stranger arrives.

6.00-6.30 News

ITV

3.30 Catch us if you can!
Part 5 of the comedy adventure. Chips and Tina stop for some fast food, but with Dervish on their trail is it fast enough?

4.00 The Name Game
The quiz show returns. Hosted by Jenny Parks.

4.30 Spitz and Spatz
Animated fun.

4.40 Story Time
Paul Hanson reads 'The Telly is Watching You' by Nicholas Fisk.

5.00 The Rikki Russell Show
Rikki and her studio guests consider the question 'Is TV bad for you?'

5.45 News and weather

6.00-6.30 It's all here!
Keep up to date with all the latest in TV, video, films, concerts and sport.

Cloud 9

3.30 Snow White and Rose Red
An animated film of the classic tale.

4.10 Mustard in the Custard
Comic verse read by Marty Hill

4.20 Grand Canyon
A film taking us from dawn to dusk in one of the world's greatest natural wonders.

5.00 News Headlines

5.05 The Ghost of Thomas Kempe
Part 2 of Penelope Lively's story.

5.30-6.30 Behind the Scenes
This edition, featuring supergroup 2 Much, won the gold award for best rockumentary in this year's World Rock Awards.

C Scanning

Scanning is looking for the information you need. Scan the TV programme listings for the answers to these questions.

1. What is on **BBC 1** at **5.00**?
2. What is on **Cloud 9** at **5.30**?
3. What is on **BBC 1** at **3.55**?
4. What is on **ITV** at **5.45**?
5. What is on **Cloud 9** at **4.10**?
6. What time does '**Spitz and Spatz**' begin?
7. What time does '**Catch us if you can!**' begin?
8. What time does '**The Book Tree**' end?
9. How long does '**Brewster's Cove**' last?
10. How many **news** programmes are listed?

D What would you watch?

Make a list of the programmes you might choose to watch from 3.30 to 6.30. Say why you have chosen each programme.

Television

Is TV Bad for You?

A What do you think?

The audience for Rikki Russell's TV show has lots of different ideas about TV.

1. List the ideas you agree with. Say why you think so.
2. List the ideas you disagree with, giving your reasons.
3. What do you think about the good and bad effects of TV?

B Your own TV discussion programme

1. Plan a group discussion on the advantages and disadvantages of TV.

These are some of the questions the presenter might ask in leading the discussion. Can you think of any others?

- Do we learn from TV? Or is it just for fun?
- Does TV encourage people to try new things, such as sports or cookery? Or do TV viewers prefer to watch others doing these things?
- What good effects has TV had on you? What bad effects do you think it might have had?
- If all the TV stations shut down today in what ways would we be better or worse off?

2. Note down your own opinions on the above questions before the discussion begins.

Planning a discussion programme

a) The presenter introduces the TV programme, and asks the opening question.
b) The presenter asks a member of the audience for his or her opinion.
c) The presenter invites other members of the audience, in turn, to comment on what has been said.
d) The presenter asks his second question, and so on.
e) The presenter brings the discussion to a close.

C Writing

1. Make notes of all the good points for TV.
2. Make notes of all its bad points.
3. Use your notes to write two paragraphs about watching TV. In the first write about its advantages, and in the second its disadvantages.

Tell Me a Story

When she reached the milestone that was halfway between her home and the town, Magpie liked to turn to look at her cottage on the hill. This time, as she was about to turn, she saw, just for a moment, a tall, noble lady waiting in the road ahead.

Magpie stiffened a little and made ready to say, 'Good day, my lady,' as she'd been taught.

But as she walked on, there was no lady at all – sunlight and shadow, a rush of wind – but no lady.

Well, that's odd,' she thought. 'I must have been dreaming.' She peered between the trees on the roadside, and looked up and down the road. Puzzled, she scratched her head and stared blankly at the ground.

Anyway, there was no carriage,' she thought. 'Such a lady would ride in a carriage.'

Then she saw a key, glinting, golden in the sunlight.

At first Magpie thought it was a penny and quickly bent to pick it up. From the moment she held the key, she knew it was special. How could something so small be so heavy? She closed her hand around the key, and still it seemed to shine. It was so beautiful, so intricately cut. It would open something very precious.

From *The Thief's Daughter* by Alan Marks

A About the story

1. Where was Magpie going? How do you know?
2. What did she think she saw?
3. Why did she think she must have been mistaken?
4. Describe the key she found.
5. What made her think it was special?
6. What do you think the key might open?

B Writing

Continue the story. Think about these questions:

- What will Magpie do with the key?
- Where will she go?
- What will she find?
- What will the key open?
- What will she find inside?
- What will happen next?
- How will the story end?

Lost and found

A Describing

These mysterious objects, long lost, have now been found.
Make a list of adjectives to describe each object. Then use the list to write a sentence or two about each one.
The first one has been done for you.

Using commas
When describing an object with more than one adjective use commas like this:
The pebble was round, smooth, cold and heavy.

glinting
golden
small
heavy
shiny
beautiful
intricately cut

The shiny golden key lay glinting in the sunlight. It was small, heavy, beautiful and intricately cut.

1

2

3

4

5

6

B Writing a story

Choose one of the objects numbered 1–6 above. Think about these questions.

- Who might it have belonged to?
- How did it become lost?
- Where did you find it?
- What is special about it?
- Will its owner try to get it back?
- What adventures will it lead you into?

Write a story about your object.

Tell Me a Story

Making Stories More Interesting

A Titles

A good title makes a reader want to read the story. Look at these titles. Choose the three which sound most interesting. For each one write the title, saying why you chose it and what kind of story you think it is.

B Covers

A book cover should catch a reader's eye.

1. Which of these covers do you think works best? Give a reason for your answer.

2. Design a new cover for a story book you have enjoyed recently.

C Beginning the story

The beginning of a story should hold a reader's attention and make him want to read on. Here are the beginnings of four stories.

a This is the story of how we became a gang of thieves. My sister Jinny says I shouldn't start like this, giving away the story in the first sentence, but I think she's wrong. If you're writing a book, you've got to make sure the right sort of people read it, haven't you? Otherwise it's not fair to them or you.

From *A Handful of Thieves* by Nina Bawden

b This is the story of the most extraordinary child who ever stuck his tongue out at the Prime Minister. His name was Nicobobinus. He lived a long time ago, in a city called Venice, and he could do anything.

From *Nicobobinus* by Terry Jones

c Last Tuesday, on his way to school, Frankie met a witch. He knew at once it would lead to trouble.

From *Flyaway Frankie* by Chris Powling

d GANG OF FOUR PRIVATE DETECTIVE AGENCY
Priya printed the words carefully in her best handwriting, in bold black felt-tip pen, on the back of an old piece of card.

From *The Phantom Knicker Nicker* by Jean Ure

1. Do you think the first sentence of *A Handful of Thieves* gives the story away? Why?
2. Do you think readers should be able to tell from the beginning if it is the right sort of book for them? Say why you think so.
3. For each of the four stories write a sentence saying what you think the story will be about.
4. Which story opening do you find the most interesting? Why?

D To think and write about

1. Which do you prefer: listening to stories, or reading them for yourself? Why?
2. What is your favourite kind of story? Why?
3. When you are choosing a story book how important to you are the following:

title?	first paragraph?
author?	type of story?
front cover?	length of story?
pictures?	

Make a list of the above in order of their importance to you, saying why you think each is important.

E Writing

Choose one of the titles in section A and use it for a story of your own.

Hurt No Living Thing

Hurt no living thing;
Ladybird, nor butterfly,
Nor moth with dusty wing.
Nor cricket chirping cheerily,
Nor grasshopper so light of leap,
Nor dancing gnat, nor beetle fat,
Nor harmless worms that creep.

Christina Rossetti

Tiniest of turtles!
Your shining back
Is a shell of orange
With spots of black.

Clive Sansom

In his black and yellow
Striped jersey he moves slowly
From flower to flower
Sucking out the honey.

Douglas Gibson

Over the pond
where the children play
I saw somebody
strange, today:
a slender, glittering,
trembling thing
with stuff like cellophane
on its wing.

Jean Kenward

A About the poems

1. Why do you think it is wrong to hurt living things?
2. Which is the only creature in Christina Rosetti's poem that doesn't have wings?
3. What insect do you think 'the tiniest of turtles' is? Give a reason for your answer.
4. What is the creature in a 'black and yellow striped jersey'? Which clues tell you?
5. What creature is the 'somebody strange'. What makes you think so?
6. Which poem do you like best? Why? Learn it by heart and recite it to the group.

What is an insect?

An insect has six jointed legs, and three parts to its body: head, thorax and abdomen.

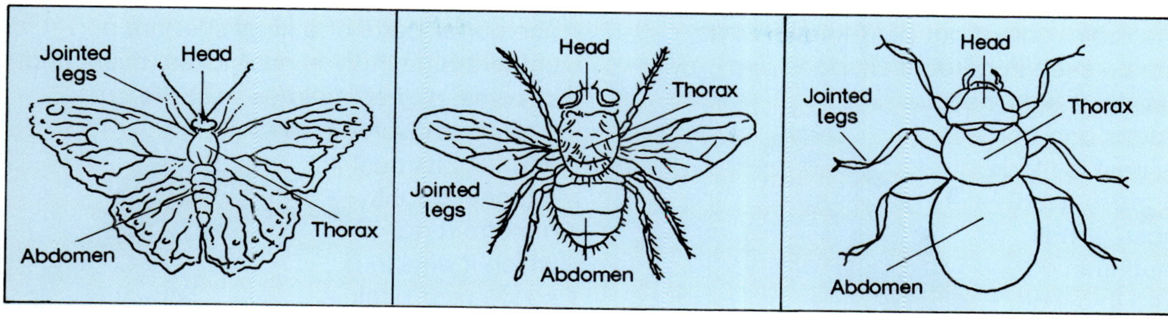

B Insects or not insects?

1. Make two alphabetical lists: **Insects** and **Not insects**.
2. Think of more small creatures to add to each list.

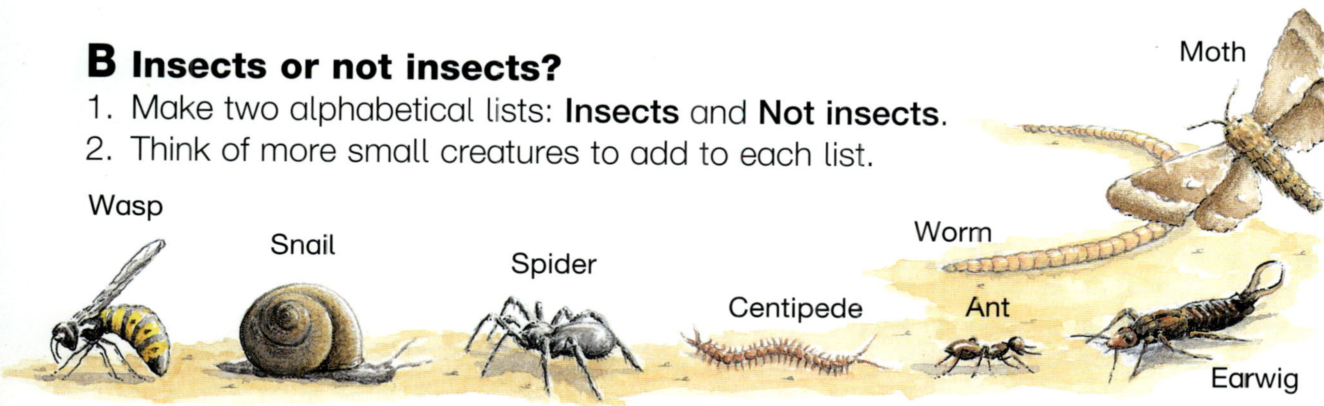

C How to draw an insect

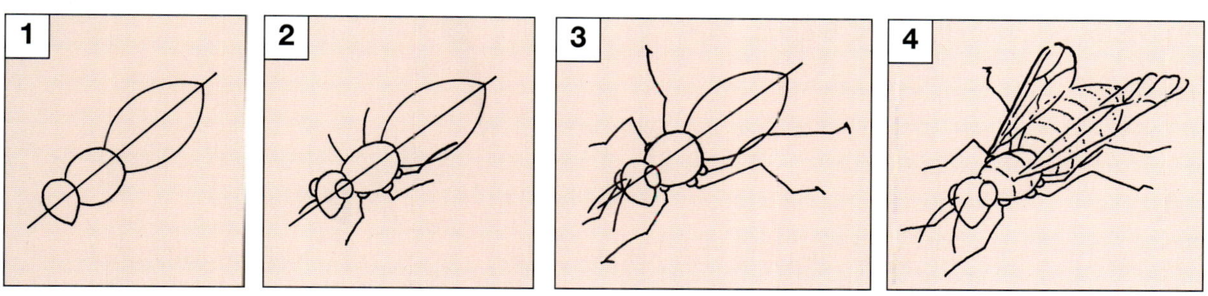

1. Use ovals for the head, thorax and abdomen, lining them up like this.
2. Draw the first part of the legs, noting carefully where they join the thorax.
3. Complete the legs. Add the antennae.
4. Draw the wings and add the rest of the detail.

Use the above guide to draw any four from your list of insects. Label your drawings to show the head, thorax and abdomen.

D Writing

Imagine you are so small that insects are as big as elephants. Write a story, explaining what happens and how you feel.

Hurt No Living Thing
British Birds

Robin (14cm)
The robin, one of our best-known birds, can be seen in gardens, hedges and woods. It eats insects, worms and berries. Its nest is made of grass, wool, moss or hair, usually in a hole in a wall, tree or bank. It lays 5-7 eggs.

Kingfisher (15-16cm)
The upper parts of a kingfisher are a brilliant blue. It lives near lakes, rivers and streams, and sometimes near the coast. It feeds on water insects and fish. Its nest is a tunnel about a metre long, which it digs in a sandy river bank. It lays 6-8 eggs on dry fish bones.

Swallow (16-22cm)
The swallow is one of our best-known summer visitors, usually seen in flight. It eats insects caught on the wing. It builds its nest of mud, on ledges in sheds or porches, laying 4-6 eggs.

A

Copy the questions. Underline the key words. Answer in complete sentences.

1. What does a swallow eat?
2. What colour is a tawny owl?
3. How many eggs does a kestrel lay?
4. What kind of nest does a kingfisher make?
5. Where does a heron build its nest?
6. What does a tawny owl feed on?
7. What is a robin's nest made of?
8. When does a bullfinch usually eat insects?
9. Which is the smallest of the birds shown?

B

Where would you expect to see:

a) a tawny owl?
b) a heron?
c) a kestrel?
d) a robin?

C

Make a list of the birds shown above in order of size (largest first).

Bullfinch (14-15cm)
The male bullfinch has a deep rose-pink breast, black head and blue-grey back. The female is duller, without the rosy breast. Bullfinches can be found in woods, bushes and orchards, where they eat seeds, berries, buds and, in summer, insects. The bullfinch lays 4-6 eggs in a nest built of twigs, roots and hair in bushes or brambles.

Kestrel (33-36cm)
Kestrels can be seen in open woods, farmland, parks, cliffs, moors and marshes. They feed on mice and insects and occasionally small birds. They build nests of sticks on a ledge or in a hole, usually in a tree or cliff, but sometimes they use the old nest of a crow, or other bird. They lay 4-5 eggs.

Tawny Owl (36-40cm)
The tawny owl is a woodland bird, rich brown in colour. It feeds at night, catching rats, mice, small birds, frogs and insects. Its nest is built of decayed wood, pellets and feathers, in holes trees, rocks, rabbit holes or chimneys. Sometimes it uses an old nest that belonged to a crow, pigeon or magpie. It lays 3-4 eggs.

Heron (90-100cm)
The heron is a tall and beautiful water bird. It often stands in shallow water watching for fish or frogs to catch. It may be found near rivers, lakes, marshes and estuaries, though its nest may be far from water. The nest is large and built of sticks, in trees, bushes, reeds, or on cliff ledges or rocks. The heron lays 3-5 eggs.

D

Answer in complete sentences.

1. How is a female bullfinch different from the male?
2. Which of the above birds eat fish?
3. Which of the above birds eat berries?
4. Which bird digs its nest?
5. In what ways are tawny owls and kestrels similar?

Hurt No Living Thing
Things To Do

A Finding out

Use your library to find answers to these questions.

1. What kind of duck is this?
   What does it eat?

2. What kind of butterfly is this?
   What kind of plant do its caterpillars feed on?

3. Find the best picture you can of the following. Write down the title and page number of the book you found it in.
   a) a grasshopper   b) a spider   c) a wasp
   d) a wasp   e) a cormorant
4. Find a good picture of a bee. Copy it carefully and label it to show the head, thorax and abdomen.
5. These are creatures from other lands. Where can they be found? What do they eat?
   a) condor   b) termite   c) green parakeet

B Riddles

Make up riddles for birds and mini-beasts to try out on your classmates. Your riddles should describe the creature and tell something else about it, such as what it eats, where it might be seen, etc. Here is one to start you off. If you are not sure check with the birds on pages 74 and 75.

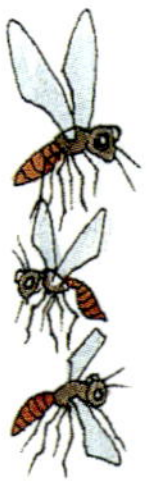

I am one of our best-known
summer visitors. I have a long
forked-tail. I catch insects as
I fly. I use mud to build my nest.
What kind of bird am I?

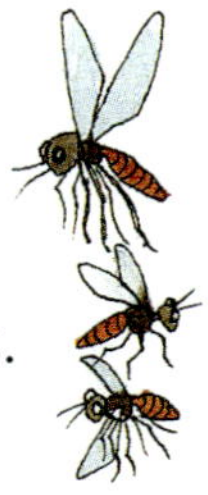

C A presentation

Prepare a one-minute talk on a bird or minibeast.
Make a list of interesting questions about it, such as:

- What does it look like?
- What does it eat?

Find out the answers and make notes. Use your notes to prepare your talk. Find or draw a picture large enough to show to the group as you talk.
Practise your talk until you are ready.

D Looking at real minibeasts

Go out into the school grounds and look for insects, spiders, worms and other minibeasts. Use small plastic boxes and tubes to collect them. Remember the poem 'Hurt No Living Thing' and handle your minibeasts with care!
Use a magnifying glass to examine each mini-beast. What colour is it? How many wings has it? How many legs? Is it an insect? Look at the way it moves.

Draw your minibeast carefully. Use reference books or a computer database to identify your minibeast. Find out about its habitat (where it lives), its food and habits. Use the books to help you label the parts of your drawing.

When you have finished your investigation release the minibeasts where you found them.

E A wormery

Make a wormery from a glass or clear plastic jar filled with alternate layers of damp soil and sand. Find two or three earthworms and place them on top of the soil. Watch to see how long they take to bury themselves. Then cover the sides of the jar with black paper held in place with elastic bands or string, otherwise the worms will stay away from the sides of the jar.

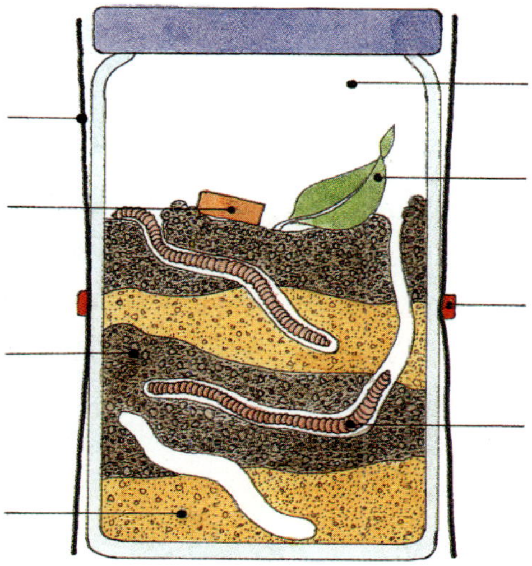

Keep the soil moist by scattering a spoonful of water over it each day. Some worms pull leaves or small pieces of apple or carrot into the soil. Put pieces of these on top of the soil to see if your worms will do so. Check the next day to see if they have.

Copy the diagram of the wormery carefully. Label it.

Answer these questions after a few days.

1. Did the worms pull any of the leaves, carrot, etc into the soil? Which did they prefer?
2. How many tunnels can you see? Where do they go?
3. Are the layers of soil becoming mixed up? Why?
4. How many worm casts can you see on top of the soil?
5. What does the wormery tell you about how worms improve soil?

How to ...

How to write

Planning

Think about your writing.
What kind of writing is it?
Why are you writing it?
Who are you writing it for?

Make notes of your ideas.

Discuss your ideas with the teacher or other children.

Choose your best ideas.

Make a plan of what you will write.

Drafting, revising and proofreading

Write a first draft.

Read what you have written.
Have you missed anything out?
Is everything in the right order?
Are there any parts which would be better left out, or could be made more interesting?

Write a second draft, putting these things right.

Proofread your work.
Are there any spelling mistakes?
Underline these and check the correct spelling.
Is the punctuation correct?
Circle any errors.

Presenting

Write a neat, correct and clear final copy.

How to learn spellings

Look, Cover, Remember, Write, Check

When you have looked up a word in a dictionary, note down its meaning and learn how to spell it.

- Look
- Cover
- Remember
- Write
- Check

How to find information

Think

What do you want to find out? Write down the **key words** in your question. Where can you find out? Which books, computer software, newspapers, etc, will help you?

Look for the key words in the index or contents. Write down the page numbers. Look for the key words on those pages.

Make notes of the information you need.

Answer your question using your notes.

Glossary

This glossary lists explanations of specialist words used in studying English. The words **in bold** in the explanations are also in the main glossary list.

abbreviation
An abbreviation is a shortened form of words.
Don't, he's; BBC, TV; Dr., Mr.; advert, telly

adjective
An adjective describes a **noun** or **pronoun**.
a ***blue*** *bus, a* ***heavy*** *box,* ***interesting*** *books*

adverb
An adverb tells us more about a verb. *He worked* ***quietly****. She picked it up* ***carefully****.*

alliteration
Alliteration is using several words together that begin with the same sound.
H*annah* ***h****urried* ***h****ome* ***h****appily.*

alphabet
The letters of the alphabet are:
a b c d e f g h i j k l m n o p q r s t u v w x y z

alphabetical order
Alphabetical order is when words are arranged in the order of the letters of the **alphabet**.
apple, banana, carrot, doughnut
When words begin with the same letter, look at the second, third or later letters to decide the right order.
bark, belong, belt, busy, butter, button

apostrophe
(**'**) an apostrophe is a raised comma. It is used for short forms of words, showing that one or more letters have been missed out.
I'm = I am: don't = do not
It is also used to show that something belongs to someone.
Elizabeth's mother, Carl's coat

author
An author is the writer of a book.

capital letter
A capital letter is used for the first word in a **sentence**, for names of people and places, and the titles of books, newspapers, plays, films, TV programmes, etc.
James, Charlie And The Chocolate Factory, Daily Mail

character
A character is a person in a story.

chapter
A chapter is a section of a book.

comma
(**,**) a comma is used to separate words in a list.
She wore an old, threadbare, woolly, red coat.
He took a drink, sandwiches, biscuits and a slice of cake.
A raised comma is known as an **apostrophe.**

consonant
A consonant is any letter that is *not* a **vowel**.
The vowels are: *a, e, i, o, u.*

contents
A contents page is a page at the front of a book that tells you what the book contains. It gives **chapter** headings and page numbers.

dictionary
A dictionary is a book in which words are listed in **alphabetical order**. It explains the meanings of the words.

exclamation
An exclamation is a **sentence** that gives a command, warning or threat. It is also used to show surprise.
Stop! What a beautiful picture!
An exclamation ends with an **exclamation mark**.

exclamation mark
(**!**) An exclamation mark is used at the end of an **exclamation**.

fiction
Fiction is stories that have been invented by the author. The books in a library are usually divided into fiction and **non-fiction** books.

full stop
(**.**) A full stop comes at the end of a **sentence** that is not a question or an exclamation.

glossary
The list you are now reading is a glossary. It is an **alphabetical** list of specialist words and their meanings. It is usually found at the back of a book.

index
An index is an **alphabetical** list of the subjects in a book, together with the pages where they can be found. An index is placed at the back of a book.

non-fiction
Non-fiction is writing that gives facts and information rather than telling a story. The books in a library are usually divided into **fiction** and non-fiction books.

noun
A noun is a naming word. Proper nouns are the special names of people and places.
Louise, Paul, Glasgow, France, Essex
Nouns that are not proper nouns are common nouns.
book, window, car, rabbit, pencil

paragraph
A paragraph is a number of **sentences** about the same subject. A new paragraph begins on a new line, and slightly in from the side of the page.

plot
The plot of a book, play, film, etc. is its story.

plural
Plural means more than one.
*apple**s**, potato**es**, bab**ies**, wol**ves***

pronoun
A pronoun is a word that stands for a **noun**.
*Jo is clever. **She** is clever. The cat scratched Ian. **It** scratched **him**.*

proofreading
Proofreading is the careful checking of a piece of written work. It means looking closely at the spelling and **punctuation**, and for ways in which you might make your work clearer or more interesting.

proverb
A proverb is a wise old saying.
Look before you leap.

punctuation
Punctuation refers to marks such as **commas, full stops, question marks, exclamation marks** and **apostrophes.**

question
A question is a **sentence** that asks for information. Questions usually begin with words such as:
Who; Whose; Why; Where; When; How
A question ends with a **question mark**.

question mark
(**?**) A question mark comes at the end of a question.

rhyme
Words that rhyme sound very similar.
cat, mat; bin, thin; sun, run

rhythm
Rhythm is a regular beat in poetry or music.

sentence
A sentence is a group of words that make complete sense. A sentence starts with a **capital letter** and ends with a **full stop, question mark** or **exclamation mark**.

setting
The setting of a book is where and when the story takes place.

singular
Singular is the form of the word that refers to just one person or thing.
apple, potato, baby, wolf

tense
Verb tense is the form of the **verb** that tells us when something happens, in the past, present or future.
Present tense: *he walks; he is walking*
Past tense: *he walked; he was walking*
Future tense: *he will walk; he will be walking*

thesaurus
A thesaurus is a book that has lists of words that have similar meaning. We use a thesaurus to help us choose more interesting words.

verb
A verb is an action word.
*He **writes**. She **jumped**. They **ran**. The dog **barked**.*

vowel
The vowels are *a, e, i, o, u*. Sometimes *y* acts as a vowel, e.g. *sp**y**; tr**y**; cr**y***

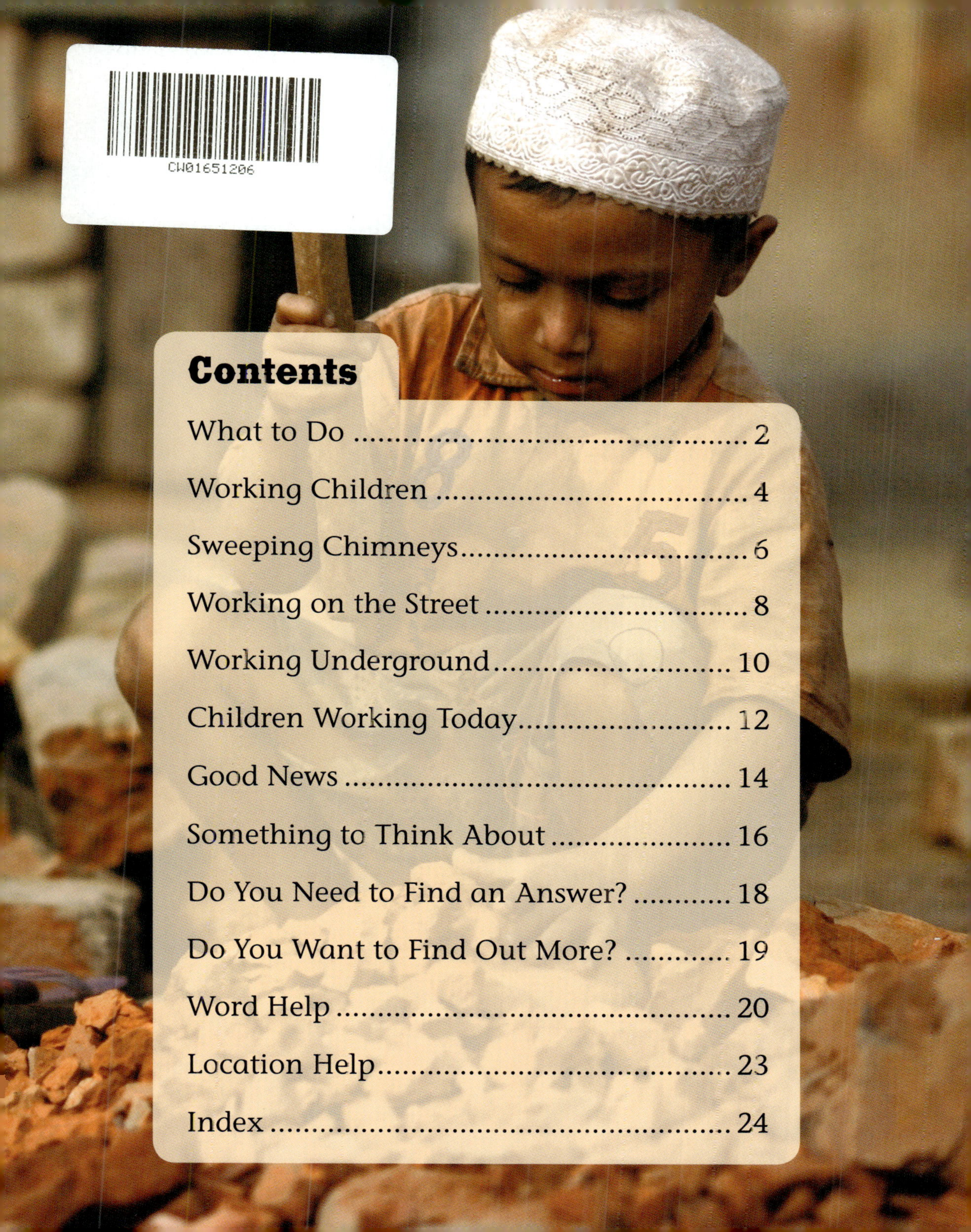

Contents

What to Do

Choose a face

Remember the colour you have chosen.

When you see your face on the page, you are the LEADER.

The LEADER reads the text in the speech bubbles.

There are extra words and questions to help you on the teacher's whiteboard. The LEADER reads these aloud.

When you see this stop sign, the LEADER reads it aloud.

You might need:

- to look at the WORD HELP on pages 20–22;
- to look at the LOCATION HELP on page 23;
- an atlas.

If you are the **LEADER**, follow these steps:

1 PREDICT

Think about what is on the page.

- Say to your group:

"I am looking at this page and I think it is going to be about . . ."

- Tell your group:

"Read the page to yourselves."

2 CLARIFY

Talk about words and their meaning.

- Say to your group:

"Are there any words you don't know?"

"Is there anything else on the page you didn't understand?"

- Talk about the words and their meanings with your group.
- Read the whiteboard.

- Ask your group to find the LET'S CHECK word in the WORD HELP on pages 20–22. Ask them to read the meaning of the word aloud.

3 ASK QUESTIONS

Talk about how to find out more.

- Say to your group:

"Who has a question about what we have read?"

- Question starters are: how..., why..., when..., where..., what..., who...
- Read the question on the whiteboard and talk about it with your group.

4 SUMMARISE

Think about who and what the story was mainly about.

When you get to pages 16–17, you can talk to a partner or write and draw on your own.

Working Children

I am looking at this page and I think it is going to be about… because…

Many years ago, some children had to work. They did not go to school. They had to work because their families were very **poor**.

The children worked long hours and they didn't get much money.

Sometimes, the work was very **dangerous**, too.

Are there any words you don't know?

Let's check: poor

Who has a question about what we have read?

How do you think the children might feel about working? Why?

These children are working in a factory.

This page was mainly about

fact

fact

STOP

My predictions were right/wrong because . . .

Sweeping Chimneys

I am looking at this page and I think it is going to be about... because...

Some children had to sweep **chimneys**.

The chimneys were not very **wide**. Sometimes, the children got stuck in them. The chimneys were dark and dirty.

Sometimes their boss lit a fire in the **grate**. This was to make the children climb faster.

Are there any words you don't know?

Let's check: grate

Who has a question about what we have read?

What sort of boss do you think the children might have had? Why?

These chimney sweeps in London have **soot** on their faces.

Working on the Street

I am looking at this page and I think it is going to be about... because...

There were many children who lived and worked on the street. They **sold** things to get money for bread. They sold **firewood** and vegetables.

Sometimes these children did jobs for **rich** people. They would clean their shoes. They would sweep the road for the rich people to cross, too.

Are there any words you don't know?

Let's check: rich

Who has a question about what we have read?

How do you know these children are poor?

A boy is cleaning shoes on the street. A girl is selling vegetables.

This page was mainly about fact fact

STOP
My predictions were right/wrong because . . .

Working Under Ground

I am looking at this page and I think it is going to be about… because…

Some children worked under the ground in **coal** mines. It was dark and wet. The children could be under ground for hours and hours. They only saw **daylight** on Sundays.

It was a very dangerous place to work, too. Sometimes, the roof of a **tunnel** would fall in.

Are there any words you don't know?

Let's check: tunnel

Who has a question about what we have read?

Why do you think they only saw daylight on Sundays?

Children could fit in the small tunnels.

This page was mainly about fact fact

STOP

My predictions were right/wrong because . . .

Children Working Still

I am looking at this page and I think it is going to be about… because...

In some places today, children still have to work. They can't go to school like most children.

Some of these children look through the **rubbish**. They look for anything they could sell to get money.

Other children do **acts**. They can dance or sing.

Some children carry things for people.

Are there any words you don't know?

Who has a question about what we have read?

Let's check: rubbish

Do you think children should be looking through rubbish? Why?

This boy finds plastic in the rubbish. He makes one **dollar** a day.

This page was mainly about fact fact

STOP
My predictions were right/wrong because . . .

Good News

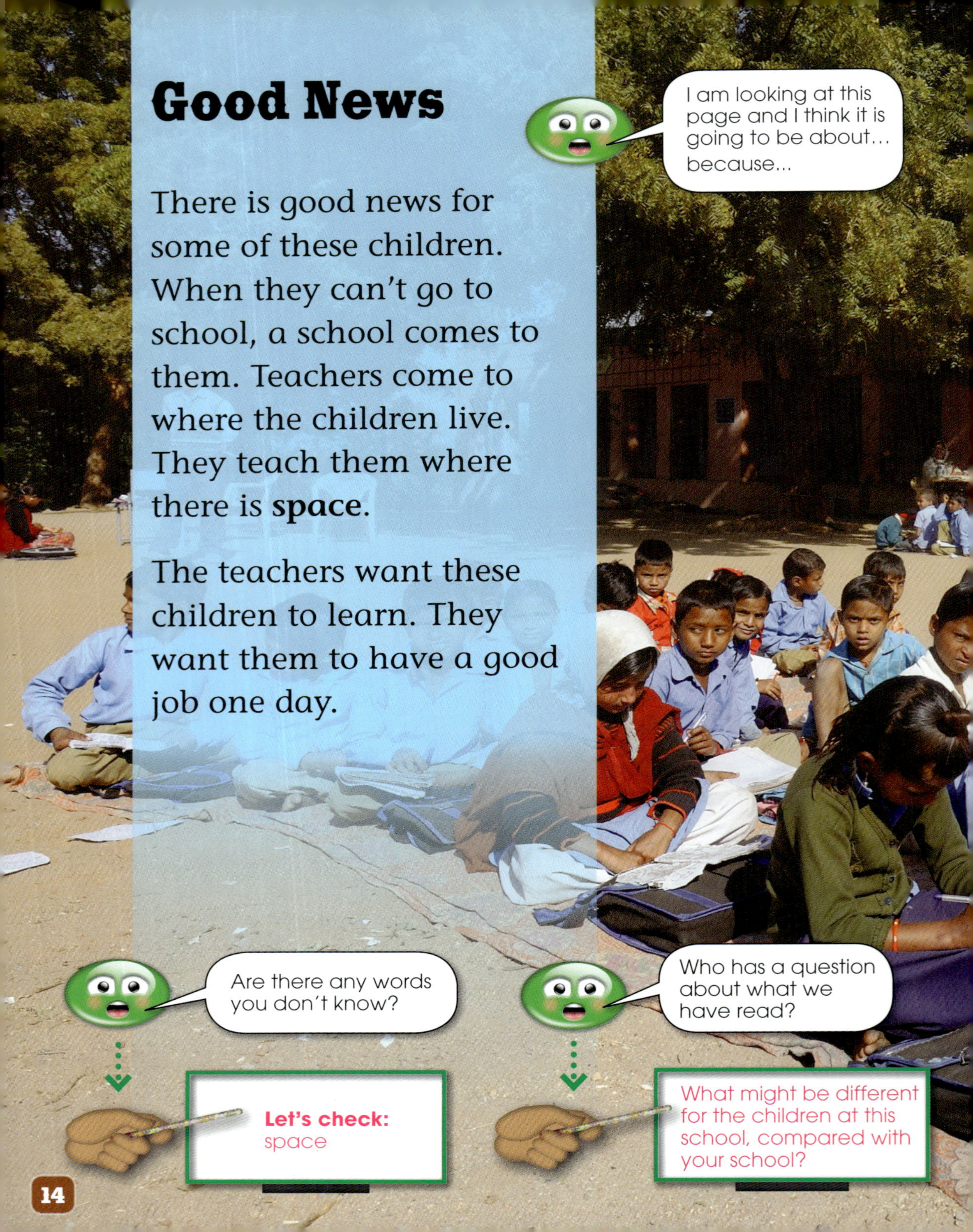

I am looking at this page and I think it is going to be about... because...

There is good news for some of these children. When they can't go to school, a school comes to them. Teachers come to where the children live. They teach them where there is **space**.

The teachers want these children to learn. They want them to have a good job one day.

Are there any words you don't know?

Let's check:
space

Who has a question about what we have read?

What might be different for the children at this school, compared with your school?

Teachers come to where the children live.

This page was mainly about fact fact

STOP

My predictions were right/wrong because . . .

Something to Think About

or

It is a good idea for children to work sometimes because...

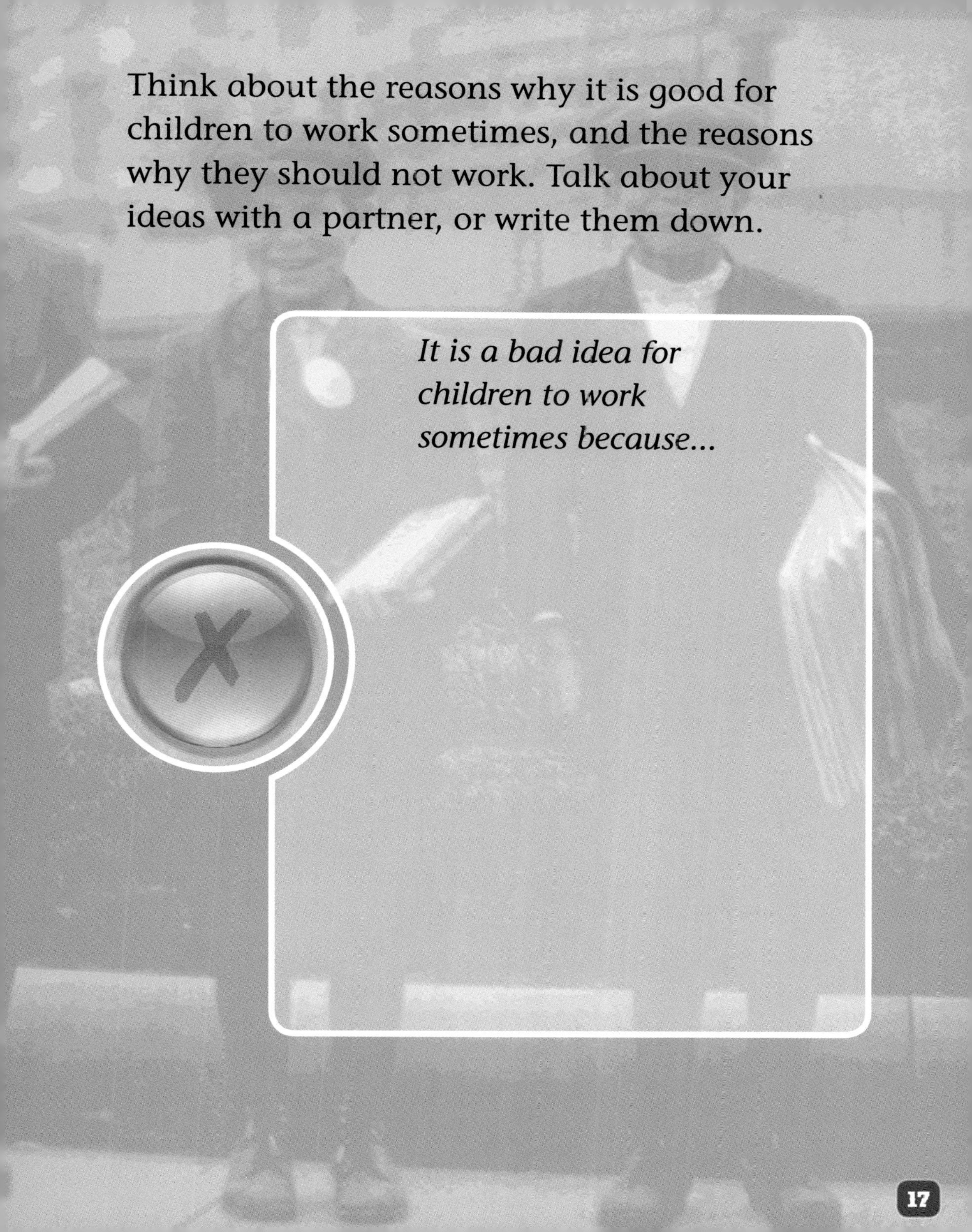

Think about the reasons why it is good for children to work sometimes, and the reasons why they should not work. Talk about your ideas with a partner, or write them down.

It is a bad idea for children to work sometimes because...

Do You Need to Find an Answer?

You could go to . . .

Do You Want to Find Out More?

You could look in books or on the internet. These key words could help you:

children in coal mines

children in factories

children in rubbish dumps

chimney sweeps

working children

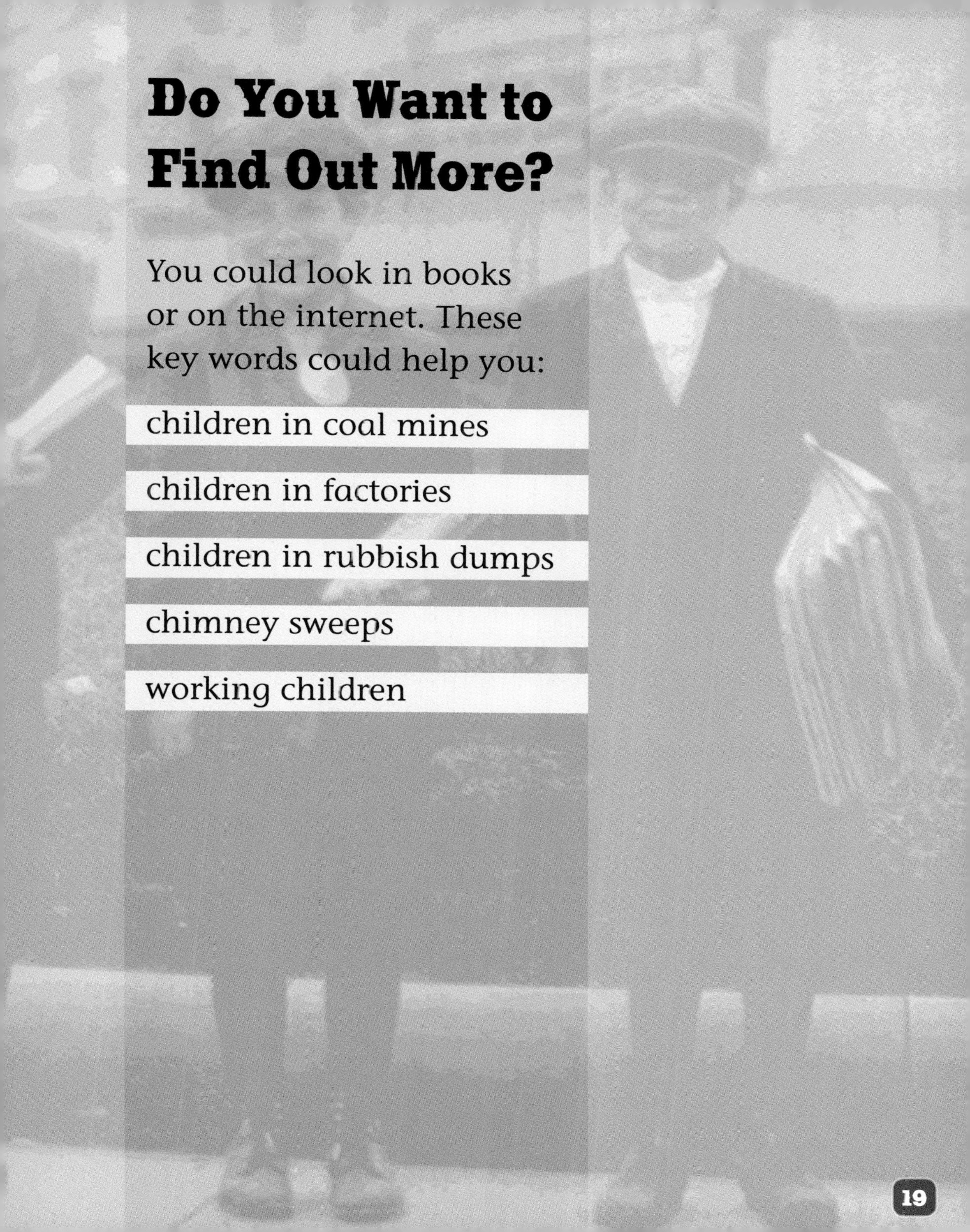

Word Help

Dictionary

acts	something like dancing or singing in front of others
chimneys	tall pipes on the top of buildings to take the smoke from fires away
coal	a part of the earth that is burned for heat
daylight	the light from the sun that we have during the day
dangerous	could kill or harm you
dollar	an amount of money used in many countries
firewood	wood that is used to burn in a fire
grate	a container made of metal bars to hold wood or coal in a fire

poor	to have little money
rich	to have a lot of money
rubbish	waste that is no longer needed
sold	gave something and got money for it
soot	black dust in chimneys from burning wood or coal
space	an open area
tunnel	a long hole that has been made under the ground or through a hill
wide	big from one side to the other side

Word Help

Thesaurus

dirty	unclean
stuck	caught
work	job

Location Help

Children Working Around the World

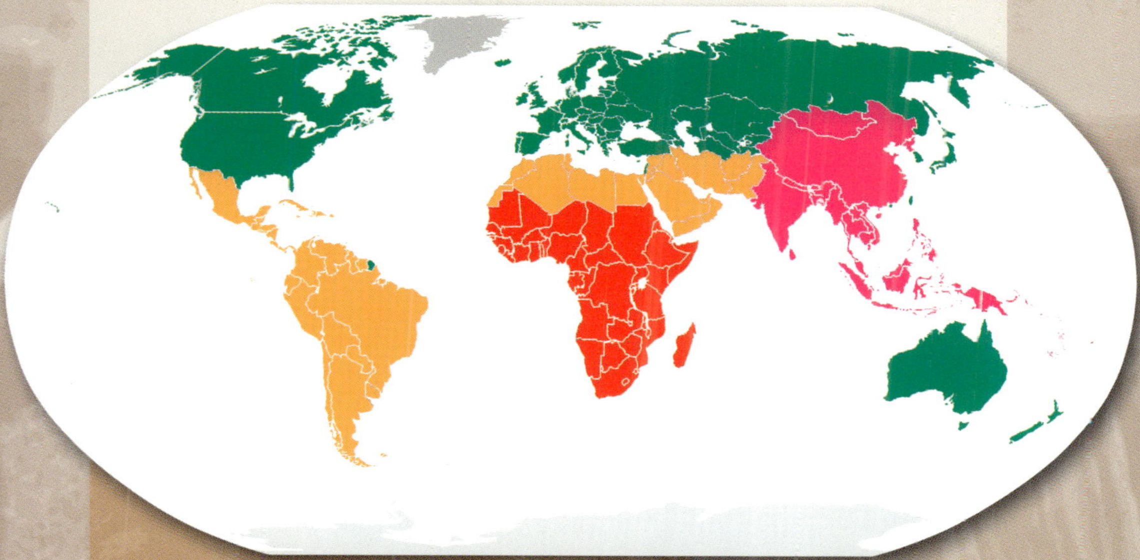

There are 211 million children who work around the world. These children are under 15 years old.

- 1 in 50 children work here*
- 1 in 14 children work here*
- 1 in 4 children work here*
- 6 out of 10 children work here*

*These numbers are from a UNICEF, UK 2005 report.

Index